Growing Critically Conscious Teachers

Growing Critically Conscious Teachers

A Social Justice Curriculum for Educators of Latino/a Youth

EDITED BY

Angela Valenzuela

National Latino/a Education
Research and Policy Project

Foreword by Sonia Nieto
Afterword by Christine Sleeter

TEACHERS COLLEGE PRESS
TEACHERS COLLEGE | COLUMBIA UNIVERSITY
NEW YORK AND LONDON

NLERAP
National Latino Education Research and Policy Project

Published simultaneously by Teachers College Press, 1234 Amsterdam Avenue, New York, NY 10027 and NLERAP, 851 S RL Thornton FWY #102, Dallas, TX 75203.

Cover art, *Cacibayagua,* by Tanya Torres. Oil on canvas, 20" × 16", 2012. Cover design by Dave Strauss.

Grateful acknowledgment is made to reprint the following:

In Chapter 6, "Our abuelos, the trees" first appeared in *This River Here: Poems of San Antonio.* San Antonio, TX: Wings Press, 2014.

In Appendix C, material modified from Flores, B., Cousin, P., & Diaz, E. (1991). Transforming deficit myths about learning, language, and culture. *Language Arts, 68*(5), 369–379.

In Appendix I, material from Productive Group Work Rubric, Doug Fisher and Nancy Frey, 2009.

In Appendix J, material from O'Hara, S., Pritchard, R., & Zwiers, Z. (2012). Identifying academic language demands in support of the Common Core Standards. *ASCD Express, 7*(17). ©2012 by ASCD.

Library of Congress Cataloging-in-Publication Data

Names: Valenzuela, Angela, editor.
Title: Growing critically conscious teachers : a social justice curriculum
    for educators of Latino/a youth / edited by Angela Valenzuela ; foreword
    by Sonia Nieto.
Description: New York, NY : Teachers College Press, [2016] | Includes
    bibliographical references and index.
Identifiers: LCCN 2015049190| ISBN 9780807756836 (pbk. : alk. paper) | ISBN
    9780807773963 (ebook : alk. paper)
Subjects: LCSH: Teachers—Training of—United States. | Hispanic
    Americans—Education. | Culturally relevant pedagogy—United States. |
    Social justice—Study and teaching—United States.
Classification: LCC LB1715 .G77 2016 | DDC 370.71/1—dc23
LC record available at http://lccn.loc.gov/2015049190

ISBN 978-0-8077-5683-6 (paper)
ISBN 978-0-8077-7396-3 (ebook)

Printed on acid-free paper
Manufactured in the United States of America

23 22 21 20 19 18 17 16   8 7 6 5 4 3 2 1

We dedicate this volume to the members of the entire NLERAP community who eagerly await this text so that they can get on with their already inspiring work of both teacher preparation and bringing others into the fold in order to cultivate the next generation of critically conscious, community-anchored, authentically caring, social justice–oriented teachers.

Sí se puede! Yes, we can!

Contents

Foreword

How to educate the growing number of Latino/a youths in the United States to become engaged, critical, and productive members of our society has been a topic of concern for educators over many decades. When I began my teaching career 50 years ago, precious few resources for teaching Latino/as existed even though in New York—where I was born and raised—we already numbered over a million and some 250,000 Latino/a children attended the city's public schools. Even at P.S. 25, the Bilingual School in the Bronx where I taught and where 85% of the students were Puerto Rican, we had negligible resources and few ideas of how to teach our students effectively. What we had were books from Spain and Mexico or translations of English language books, none of which were relevant to our mostly Puerto Rican urban students. Multicultural education, culturally responsive and social justice education, Participatory Action Research (PAR), Critical Race Theory (CRT), and other theories and approaches were not to appear for several decades.

Those of us who began our teaching careers a number of decades ago—even Latin@s—had little idea of where to find appropriate resources, or how to prepare lessons that fully engaged our students, taking into account their native languages and cultures, as well as their lived realities. It is in this context that *Growing Critically Conscious Teachers: A Social Justice Curriculum for Educators of Latino/a Youth* will make an enormous contribution to the field. It will also be a cherished resource and guide for Latin@ and non-Latin@ teachers alike, and for the university faculty and school- and community-based facilitators who help prepare them. As such, it is a welcome addition to the small but growing literature on educating Latin@ students in U.S. schools.

This volume is unique for a number of reasons. First, although it is a "handbook," it is not what we usually think of as a handbook.

Rather than prescriptive recipes for curriculum or pedagogy, it is more like a toolbox that includes history, theories, strategies and resources to assist educators in becoming knowledgeable and competent guides for Latin@ students. At the same time, it will help policymakers rethink some of the more onerous policies that have defined public education in the past three decades, policies that have done little to improve educational outcomes for Latin@ students.

Significantly, this book also emphasizes a "grow your own" approach to changing the demographics of the teaching profession. Through no fault of their own, countless Latin@s in communities around the country have been the victims of inferior schooling. Given their lack of opportunities, it is no surprise that the number of Latino/a teachers in our nation's schools is appallingly small. Yet their experiences, insights, and talents will continue to be wasted if we do not take advantage of what they offer our children. Moreover, for any number of reasons Latin@s who have succeeded in school have not often considered teaching as a profession they might want to enter. This book offers strategies for community colleges, universities, and school districts to help make teaching more enticing and bring more Latin@s into teaching through innovative and long-term projects that can change the complexion of the teaching profession.

At the same time that *Growing Critically Conscious Teachers* describes a "grow-your-own" philosophy, it also recognizes that teachers of all backgrounds can benefit from becoming aware of, and comfortable with, strategies that focus on culturally relevant pedagogy and curriculum. It recognizes that as our society changes, becoming more diverse than ever before, it is the responsibility of all educators—teachers, administrators, teacher educators, and policymakers—to adapt not only their practices but also their attitudes and dispositions to best educate the children in our classrooms both now and in the future.

The history of NLERAP is also briefly chronicled in this volume, giving readers insight into how NLERAP itself has been a "grow-your-own" project that began with the vision of educator Pedro Pedraza and has continued under the able leadership of Angela Valenzuela. These educators, and the others who have participated in this project since its inception as well as those newer to it, believe wholeheartedly in the importance of stepping up to teach our own young people with love, empathy, and consistency, and also in properly preparing those who will teach them. The participants who have lent their expertise to this volume are impressive for their experience and knowledge.

Known nationally and internationally for their efforts on behalf of Latin@ students as well as for their research and advocacy, the contributors represent some of the most significant scholars in the field.

Rarely has one book included so many of the concepts and themes that are the bedrock of critical teaching today. Incorporating Vygotskian perspectives, Critical Race Theory (CRT), social justice education, Participatory Action Research (PAR), critical pedagogy, and sample curricula and bibliographies, this book will serve as a model not only for educating teachers of Latino/a students, but for educating teachers of all students. While the book focuses on the unique historical and sociocultural realities of Latin@s in terms of the principles it espouses, its reach is potentially universal.

Finally, this volume is unique in that it considers not only educators' dispositions and knowledge, but also the policies at school, city, state, and federal levels that can either hinder or support student learning. Some of these policies are based on a lack of understanding of the sociocultural realities of Latin@ youths and communities; others are based on scant awareness of the kinds of approaches that might work best for Latin@ students. But some derive directly from the xenophobic attitudes that have led to misguided policies such as the downsizing or even the elimination of approaches like bilingual education, an approach that has been found time and again to be successful in promoting the achievement of Latin@ and other students learning English. Thus this book challenges not only these negative aspects, but also the limited policies that result from them. Scripted curricula, rigid accountability for both teachers and students, the privatization and corporatization of public schooling, inflexible ability group tracking, obsessive high-stakes testing, and negative deficit discourses, among other policies and decisions, have gotten in the way of quality education for Latin@ students. *Growing Critically Conscious Teachers* asks us to take a step back and reconsider what education for Latino/a, and indeed *all* students, should really be about.

Sonia Nieto
Professor Emerita, Language, Literacy, and Culture
College of Education
University of Massachusetts, Amherst

Acknowledgments

Although the authors involved first began the actual writing process for this book in the summer of 2012 as part of a Kellogg-funded grant to develop the curriculum herein, the process occurred much earlier under a grant from the Ford Foundation that funded our Grow Your Own Teacher Education Institutes initiative. Hence, we, as the National Latino/a Education Research and Policy Project (NLERAP), are extremely grateful to both foundations for giving us this opportunity. We are also indebted to the University of Texas at Austin for a subvention grant that helped us bring this volume to fruition.

I give thanks to Patricia D. López, former NLERAP associate director, for her editorial suggestions and commentary on the earliest stages of the first chapter. Speaking on behalf of all of the contributors to this volume, I also want to thank her for playing a key and invaluable role in helping us to organize our thoughts through the initial outlines. Thanks, as well, to Úrsula Casanova and Kathy Mooney, who edited this volume at its early and later stages, respectively. Brenda Rubio also provided help with appendices at a crucial moment. Specific thanks go to the members of NLERAP's Curriculum and Participatory Action Research Committees, respectively, for dedicating so many hours to this collective writing effort that also produced a volume on participatory action research, titled *PAR Entremundos: A Pedagogy of the Américas* (Ayala, Cammarota, Rivera, Rodriguez, Torre, & Berta-Avila, forthcoming). These committees consist of Barbara Flores, Jennifer Ayala, Julio Cammarota, Melissa Rivera, Louie Rodriguez, María Torre, Margarita Berta-Avila, and Adele Arellano. We all gathered in New York, Dallas, Sacramento, and Austin—some places more than once—to engage in deep, focused dialogues on what it means to be community-engaged, Latino/a scholars who work at the intersections of teacher preparation, policy, pedagogy, action research, and practice, and how these dialogues were to find expression in both volumes.

Thanks to Carmen Mercado for contributing to this volume and giving us the language we needed to make the theoretical case for the crucial role of the teacher as extending beyond knowledge and skills to include dispositions. Thanks to Pedro Pedraza and Sonia Nieto for providing critical reviews of the manuscript in its earliest stages, as well as to Sonia Nieto and Christine Sleeter, respectively, for writing the Foreword and Afterword to this volume.

Special thanks, as well, to Puerto Rican artist Tanya Torres, who gifted us with the image for our book cover, entitled *La Cacibayagua*. According to Taíno mythology, Cacibayagua is a cave that is physically located in the Dominican Republic that gives birth to the Taíno people, and with it, a consciousness that, in Torres's words, is rooted in an awareness of "the Earth as Mother." To this, she adds, "I thought the cave Cacibayagua, from which the Taínos are said to have come, might be a place of earth and river water from whose veins flows life. Cacibayagua is earth, and she is also water. Like the Black Virgin, she is the color of the Earth. Water, cave, virgin goddess, like the ancient Goddess, mother of all." (Torres, 2015). Symbolically, *La Cacibayagua* portrays on canvas much of what this volume also attempts to convey—but which each reader must discover on her or his own.

Given our elder epistemology (Gonzales, 2015), it is fitting to acknowledge NLERAP region heads and national leaders, Hector M. Flores and Dr. Luis Antonio ("Tony") Baez, for their words of wisdom that have remained with us throughout:

"The teaching profession is the most important profession of all because it is the key to all the other professions." (Flores, 2012)

"The best curriculum is written in times of struggle." (Baez, 2013)

Their words have held deep resonance for us. We are grateful to them and all of our elders and broader NLERAP community for holding on to the dream of a revived, democratic vision for public education and for reminding us that we ourselves are the collective embodiment of this much-needed change for our schools and society. Pedro Pedraza and Melissa Rivera deserve enormous credit, as well, for founding NLERAP in 2000. Finally, at Teachers College Press, Marie Ellen Larcada, who has since retired, deserves a lot of credit for encouraging us to make this happen. Brian Ellerbeck and Sarah Biondello have also been wonderful in helping to bring this volume to fruition. It takes a village, indeed!

—A.V.

Preface
Uses of the Handbook

This handbook is born out of the collective efforts of the National Latino/a Education Research and Policy Project (NLERAP, pronounced "nel-rap"). It brings together our collective best thinking on how our higher education institutions can best teach the future teachers of Latina and Latino youth specifically, but also children of color and language-minority youth, in general, in our nation's secondary schools. Although this handbook on secondary teacher preparation is specifically born out of our own national Grow Your Own Teacher Education Institutes (GYO-TEI) initiative (discussed fully in Chapter 1), it will nevertheless resonate with a significant and growing body of scholarship that underscores the importance of sociocultural and sociopolitical perspectives in teaching and learning. It will also resonate with audiences wanting to develop community-based school and district partnerships that are also philosophically place-based. That is, they simultaneously develop pathways into the teaching profession while grounding children and youth to themselves, each other, and their communities through the curriculum advanced herein. In this vein, we hope that the participatory action research (PAR) approach to teacher preparation that we espouse will inspire, motivate, and provide tangible direction for a social justice approach to teacher preparation, within which it can and should optimally be embedded.

This volume stresses the importance of teachers' dispositions in the educational process at the same time that it points structurally to the viability of a partnership model or approach for carrying out a "grow your own" (GYO) initiative. With respect to the former, this volume provides overarching topics, themes, frameworks, and instructional activities that readers—most especially university faculty

Although this is by no means a how-to text on establishing your own
GYO-TEI initiative, it is nevertheless suggestive of key elements, the
most important of which may be intentionality and good will with a
stakeholder community or budding partnership that is willing to do the
hard work of coming into conversation to discuss values, needs, approaches, resources, and requisite relationships for laying the ground-
work for a GYO initiative. Just as importantly, this volume provides
readers with a higher education teacher preparation curriculum that
is further grounded in the actual work that we do at our respective
GYO-TEI sites.

With respect to building a pathway for teachers, years of investment in developing an infrastructure has shown us the extent to
which this is an extremely involved and complex enterprise. We have
also learned that there is no one way. Consider applying our ideas
to your context by forming partnerships; offering courses that align
to the themes, readings, and exercises that we impart; and growing
your own critically conscious teachers. The arrangements you devise
will, of necessity, take different shapes and forms, depending on your
context.

As for the research component, the possibilities are limitless. PAR
is of obvious relevance to any GYO effort that incorporates this as a
key component. Just as importantly, evaluation and capacity building
are ever-present needs. Goals, targets, desired outcomes, and ways
to measure these help determine the relative success, opportunities,
and challenges of the overall initiative. Research-practice partnerships
that provide a specific focus on practitioners provide another avenue
for useful research by contributing to the accumulation of knowledge
about education policy and practice.

The long-term sustainability of any GYO venture would further
benefit greatly from in-depth investigations of school, neighborhood,
and district contexts. It would build on the actual work of the partnership to illuminate understandings of policies, resources, practices, beliefs, and demographic shifts and how these impact the initiative and
the work of the partnership. What is potentially most rewarding about
this as a researcher is the opportunity to establish a field research site
in a geographically proximate community that you ostensibly serve,
but may actually know little about—at least not in any in-depth manner. In short, research strengthens and legitimizes the work of the

partnership. Should you have questions in this regard, feel free to contact us at NLERAP.org for a consultation so that we may offer suggestions, advice, and guidance, accordingly, along any of these lines.

Reflected in this text is our individual and collective expertise in cultivating future secondary teachers of Latino/a youth that grows out of our own prolonged engagement with this population as community advocates, researchers, university faculty, and published scholars. Although NLERAP scholars have been researching and writing individually for many years in the areas of teacher preparation, cultural studies in education, and culturally and linguistically responsive pedagogy, coalescing our work into this handbook has been a groundbreaking endeavor that involved lengthy hours of conversations and meetings over an extended period of time and that continues into the present.

Chapter 1, "True to Our Roots: NLERAP and the Grow Your Own Teacher Education Institutes Initiative," presents the reader with our guiding metaphor, *El Árbol* (The Tree), to describe our origins, our political genealogy, and the structure of our organization. It also brings research evidence to bear on why, as a country, growing our own teachers makes sense. Chapter 2, "Teacher Capacities for Latino and Latina Youth," examines research evidence on teacher capacities as extending beyond knowledge and skills to also consist of dispositions. Even if they are frequently overlooked in conventional treatments of teacher capacities, dispositions are essential to both to community-oriented teaching and student success. Chapter 3, "Teaching for Critical Consciousness: Topics, Themes, Frameworks, and Instructional Activities," is organized around seven topics that the reader will find useful for teaching from a sociocultural, sociopolitical, and social justice paradigm. It is the culmination of many months of dialogue and sharing the best of what our NLERAP scholars have to offer our nation's teacher preparation classrooms, where cultivating critically conscious practitioners is an explicit goal. Chapter 4, "*PAR Entremundos*: A Practitioner's Guide," examines the philosophical roots and guiding principles of participatory action research (PAR), with an eye toward making these tangible to practitioners. This, too, was the culmination of many months of collaboration among members of NLERAP's Participatory Action Research Committee. They sought to make explicit the philosophical and practical components of PAR in the context of teacher preparation. Chapter 5, "Social Justice Education Project (SJEP): A Case Example of PAR in a High School Classroom," takes the reader through an entire PAR process based on an actual classroom experience of the Social Justice Education Project in Tucson, Arizona. Chapter 6, "Conclusion: *El Árbol*/The Tree: Returning to the Root," takes the reader back to the beginning of the volume to underscore anew how metaphor—specifically *El Árbol*/The Tree— offers us new language, symbols, and, as a consequence, thought processes through which to articulate a fresh, hopeful vision of education for our nation.

To the reader: I would ask that you read the book from front to back. The reason is that a core idea of this manuscript is the importance of fostering successive generations of future teachers who possess not only the requisite knowledge and skills, but, most especially, the dispositions they need in order to make a difference in their culturally diverse classrooms. Without giving too much away, these dispositions are arguably acquired as much through reading, reflection, and practice as through lived experience in the context of moral, progressively minded communities. So consider taking your time to savor this handbook so that you might derive maximum benefit.

Growing Critically Conscious Teachers

CHAPTER 1

True to Our Roots

NLERAP and the Grow Your Own Teacher Education Institutes Initiative

Angela Valenzuela

INTRODUCTION

Cognizant of our historical situatedness as Latina and Latino faculty, researchers, and advocates of color—as well as of teachers in higher education institutions—we are mindful, even as we are distasteful, of the prevailing factory models, mechanistic metaphors, and concomitant approaches that characterize much public education in the United States today (Santa Ana, 2002). We share the view that our students need literacies that empower them (Macedo, 2006; Macedo, Dendrinos, & Gounari, 2003). By this we mean a kind of education that fully promotes their bicultural and biliteracy potentialities and competencies that further promote critical thinking, allowing them to form their own opinions based on what they read, research, and analyze as opposed to what they are told. We share a collective concern with how the current "subtractive schooling" framework finds expression in our state- and federally mandated high-stakes accountability systems—and in so doing, potentially robs them of an opportunity for empowerment and self-actualization (Valenzuela, 1999). Accordingly, we deliberately challenge this conceptualization with a metaphor of our own, namely, *El Árbol* (The Tree), which has come to hold special meaning for us in the National Latino/a Education Research and Policy Project (NLERAP, pronounced "nel-rap").

We begin by explaining the reasons underlying our choice of *El Árbol* as a guiding metaphor for our initiative. It helps convey the idea that this curriculum handbook is intended not only to impart critical understandings, knowledge, and agency for the future teachers of our growing Latino demographic, but also to inspire a deeply rooted sense of history premised on a "generational consciousness," or what we might term an "ancestral praxis" (Gonzales, 2015; Moreno Sandoval, 2013).

This narrative has direct bearing on what we are attempting to accomplish, nationally, in our own specific efforts—most particularly, NLERAP's Grow Your Own Teacher Education Institutes (GYO-TEI) initiative. We explain the grassroots and grasstops organizational structure through which our work is carried out, which then segueways into the following sections that address the research base that informs the GYO-TEI initiative. This narrative highlights the important role that community, university, and school and district partnerships play—or can play, as the case may be—in the formation of our secondary Latina/o teacher preparation pathway into higher education.

OUR GUIDING METAPHOR: *EL ÁRBOL*

El Árbol is an appropriate metaphor for NLERAP's national Grow Your Own Latino/a Teacher Initiative, an organization that, while rooted in disparate histories of struggle, has coalesced and sprung branches throughout the years. Describing NLERAP using *El Árbol* draws attention to the deep-rooted sense of interconnectedness and empowerment that undergirds NLERAP's defining GYO-TEI initiative, and thus this volume. *El Árbol* stands for our shared history; our dense, interconnected branches; and the accumulation of strength, knowledge, experience, and wisdom that informs this handbook.

Whereas *árboles* (trees, or "family trees") are typically associated with genealogies of biological lineages, political genealogies refer to direct linkages between contemporary organizations and earlier institutions and organizations, and the political identities that they have engendered. As discussed later in the chapter, these linkages capture the depth of our sense of identity as an organization that is itself already 15 years old, without including either the many longer-term relationships enjoyed by many of our members or its earlier history that extends this lineage to 32 years and counting. This generational consciousness of our own history inspires the thought that we are the literal progeny not only of our biological and political lineages, but also of very rich, deep histories and legacies that connect us all to one another and that are responsible for the very opportunities and privileges that we collectively share today—including the opportunity of a joint experience to write this volume.

Although one may question whether a metaphor can be taken too far, both the symbolic power of trees for humans and the different thought process and emergent constructive discourse that *El Árbol* inspires are compelling. To wit, in the Kilongo Bantu language, *muntu* is a word that for certain trees means both "tree" and "person," as well as "ancestors" (Jahn & Grene, 1961). Similarly, the term *yaxche-baalche* in Mayan philosophy conveys both "trees" and "human beings." Because the tree is the ultimate symbol of life for the Maya, the death of the last tree equates to the death of the last human being (Cintli Rodriguez, 2014). Similarly, in English and Spanish, respectively, we are familiar with the phrases *tree of life* and *el árbol de la vida*.

In English and Spanish, we approximate these combined meanings when we speak of "family trees," "trunks," "roots," and "branches," and when we insure ourselves against the "the risk of loss of life and limb." We also have sayings such as "A chip off the old block," and its rough equivalent in Spanish, *"De tal palo, tal astilla"*; and we use words such as *wooden*, and its Spanish equivalent *acartonado*, to mean "expressionless" (*carton* refers to a paper product). Our brains, arguably our most important body organ, are connected to a "stem" or "trunk," a *tronco* in Spanish. Here are many other tree-related words and phrases that are commonly used to describe the kind of efforts that characterize our GYO-TEI initiative:

nurture	cultivate	grounded
fertile	harvest	organic
seeds	branches	roots/rootedness
grassroots	grasstops	root causes

Warren and Mapp (2011) utilize the metaphor of the tree in their book, *A Match on Dry Grass: Community Organizing as a Catalyst for School Reform*, to symbolize how educational political activism is rooted in preexisting political identities. According to Delgado-Bernal (2001), political identities originate in the home; and according to Valenzuela (1999), such identities may be interpersonally expressed as *"ser bien educado,"* or "being well educated," in the Latino sense (Valenzuela, 1999). Roots also serve as metaphors for memory and the historical experience of colonization that began over 500 years ago with Columbus's arrival to this hemisphere, resulting in enduring trauma that continues into the present (Cintli Rodriguez, 2014; Galeano, 1997).

In a path-breaking novel titled *El Mesquite: A Story of the Early Spanish Settlements Between the Nueces and the Rio Grande*, written and published in 1935 by Elena Zamora O'Shea (reprinted in 2000), the tree itself is the novel's personified narrative voice. At an earlier time when women—especially Mexican American women—had precious little voice, Zamora O'Shea was able to ingeniously overcome this by narrating the history of the *ranchero* (or ranch) culture in South Texas of the 1880s and 1890s that passed under the branches of that ancient tree. In so doing, she recovers an otherwise uprooted history and offers in its stead a sense of renewal for the ages by re-rooting it and promoting an enduring sense of place, identity, and legacy in the South Texas soil.

What came to be known as the "Conquest of the Americas" is a necessary touchstone for understanding the education of Latina/o youth, historically. Renowned Native American poet Simon Ortiz (1993) speaks to his own experiences that, unfortunately, continue to resonate with those of so many youth today:

> I felt an unspoken anxiety and resentment against unseen forces that determined our destiny to be un-Indian, embarrassed and uncomfortable with our grandparents' customs and strictly held values. We were to set our goals as American working men and women, single-mindedly industrious, patriotic, and unquestioning, building for a future which ensured that the U.S. was the greatest nation in the world. I felt fearfully uneasy with this, for by that I felt the loneliness, alienation, and isolation imposed on me by the separation from my family, home, and community. (p. 34)

Although Ortiz, a Pueblo Indian, actually had to leave home and family in the 1950s to attend boarding school in Santa Fe and in Albuquerque, every day in America, children are still required to "leave home," albeit symbolically, because of the culturally chauvinist curriculum to which they are routinely subjected, and most typically by teachers and school systems that systematically fail to construct a meaningful educational practice out of students' languages, cultures, community-based identities, or real-world experiences. Hence, we witness alienation and disaffection from schooling for so many U.S. minority youth (Valenzuela, 1999), an experience frequently matched by the alienation of teachers of color (Achinstein & Ogawa, 2011; Carr & Klassen, 1997; Gursky, 2002; Matias, 2013).

According to a comparative, large-scale study that measures academic success from the lens of intergenerational mobility with respect to high school graduation and college attainment, Mexican American children—and analogously other under privileged Latinos—are extraordinarily successful (Lee & Zhou, 2014). The "problem" of Latino underachievement is not about their lack of any particular trait or a devaluing of education. With very few exceptions, all parents value and care about their children's education. Rather, the issue is parents' low educational attainment levels that make it difficult for them to translate their caring into practices that promote achievement (Lee & Zhou, 2014; Valenzuela, 1999).

Further complicating matters is an ongoing tawdry history of colonization and Americanization (also called assimilation), the schooling of Latina and Latino children and youth—and children of color, generally—is characteristically vexed. The Latino folk model of education, or *educación*, is simply invisible (Bartlett & Garcia, 2011; Riley, 1993; Valenzuela, 1999). Rather than being based on official definitions, folk models originate from the lived practices and knowledge of a community (Moll, 1998). Latinos' folk model calls upon them to live in the world neither as "empty vessels" to be filled with knowledge, nor as the intellectually, morally, socially, or culturally deficient individuals that schools and society frequently make them out to be. Instead, they are to live as social, responsible, caring, and respectful human beings, observing and honoring the dignity of others (Valenzuela, 1999; Valdés, 1996). Hernandez's (1993) words ring sadly, if hopefully, true:

> I would venture to say that he [Ortiz] and all of the rest of us who have survived have called on every ounce of our originality to give us the strength and inspiration for what Ortiz calls our "fight back." This originality is found in the original cultural teachings that honor our humanity, our dignity, and our spirits as necessary components of our identity. (p. 11)

We, too, seek to cultivate this "fight back" in the next generation of critically conscious teachers. By this, we mean a voice that courageously and intelligently stands up against injustice and does so from a culturally and community-anchored standpoint.

As this volume outlines in greater detail in Chapter 2, today's focus on developing teachers' knowledge and skills manages to miss the mark. Among other things, it reinstantiates the Cartesian mind–body split that exists in Western culture (Daza & Huckaby, 2014).

This long-standing fetishizing of the mind sets us up for a conversation about education that privileges and valorizes individual merit and achievement, champions false notions of entitlement, promotes mental testing, and endorses uninspiring educational reforms to narrow the "achievement gap." Limiting and frequently toxic, this discourse is diversionary. At worst, it robs students of *la buena educación*—a virtuous education—precisely because it fails to build additively on students' capacities that are lodged in an understanding of our diverse histories as Latinas and Latinos in the United States, together with a critical understanding of contemporary forms of oppression and our responses to it.

I do not at all suggest that student achievement gaps and outcomes are unimportant, but rather that the *discourses* surrounding them are limiting. This text does not address, in an in-depth manner, the problem of Latino underachievement, other than to note that ample research exists showing that Latino students are performing at or near the bottom on every achievement measure (Gándara & Contreras, 2009), including high school graduation (Orfield, Losen, Wald, & Swanson, 2004). Although Gándara and Contreras (2009) note multiple factors that are responsible for Latinos' low achievement levels—including underfunded schools, parents' education levels, poverty, high-stakes testing, access to quality teaching and teachers, and hyper-segregation—they are particularly critical of state and federal policies that translate into a chronic underinvestment in this community. Menken (2008) and Pandya (2011) offer comprehensive critical examinations of the ways that English learners are particularly negatively impacted by our current framework of high-stakes testing and accountability.

Education is about people. It is about how we as individuals and as members of moral communities move and get on in the world. You might ask what motivates and drives us to dedicate our lives to the study of education, and now to carry out this national effort in which you may be poised to participate. Accordingly, *El Árbol* helps us to articulate this deeper dimension of our work. We are a collective of critical scholars who seek an emancipatory approach to education. Accordingly, we aim to nurture a capacity for renewal not only for the students in our classrooms, but also for our children, communities, teachers, and ourselves.

If we ourselves are not renewed by our own efforts, how can we possibly expect our teachers and children to thrive? Indeed, we must rediscover and reinvent education in and for our times, together with fresh articulations of the good, the true, and the beautiful (Becker, 1967). We embrace the notion that love of self, family, and community promotes a healthy sense of pride and dignity upon which a solid foundation for a strong and meaningful life can rest. At its best, *la buena educación* inspires a high sense of purpose and a transcendent view of personhood and basic human dignity.

Although romantic representations of trees tend to convey vibrant, sensual presences, together with geometric patterns against a panorama of landscape imagery, NLERAP particularly identifies with trees' extraordinary subterranean root systems—less visible, but no less potent or awe-inspiring. These dense underground networks signify our biological, spiritual, intellectual inheritances, organizing traditions, and political identities and genealogies that have found expression in our protracted social, legal, and political struggles for civil and human rights.

Philosophically, the idea of an "authentic" Latina or Latino is anathema to us. We emanate from or inhabit geographic borderlands that require us to navigate, negotiate, and express ourselves as Chicanas or Latinas in the contradictory and ambiguous space that is unique to the borderland (Anzaldúa, 2007; also see Cotera, 1976; Mireles & Cotera, 2006). Identity is therefore never static but always shifting, multilayered, and contextual, related to macro-level demographic categories (e.g., "Latina," "Latino," "Hispanic") as well as to local, ethnographically specific identities (e.g., "Boricua," "Nuyorican," "Chicana," "Tejana," "Tejano").

There is no mythic or essentialist Latino identity to discover or go back to (Gutiérrez & Rogoff, 2003). Rather, our identities are overwhelmingly informed by a shared experience of oppression, a shared sense of fate, and a potentially deep connection to this continent, our ancestral home (Valenzuela, Zamora, & Rubio, 2015).

At times, *El Árbol* is abundantly adorned, its branches full of leaves that provide protective shade or shelter; at other times, it stands bare, weathering harsh environmental conditions. Yet year after year, it regenerates. A parallel process occurs with NLERAP. Our emphasis on the importance of remaining rooted in our communities positions us well for survival. It provides us with a grounded sense of identity that helps us to differentiate between traditions, beliefs, and practices that are essential to our pursuit of social justice and those that undermine our efforts. It also helps us to recognize a good idea when we hear it.

Perhaps most importantly, the structure of our organization (described further in a later section) promotes an invaluable intergenerational perspective of knowledge that is lodged in a sense of history—past, present, and future. Hernandez (1993) expresses this sense well: "I have heard many elders say that we that walk the earth now are the link between our ancestors and our unborn generations— the past and the future come together in us" (p. 11). In this view, the burden of members of the current generation is to not simply anticipate the life chances of the members of the next, but to actually shape them through the passing down of a way of being in the world—as critical educators with the requisite capacities enhanced by the gift of their own personal histories and stories, so that they and their families and communities may achieve stable, fulfilling lives.

Another reason we embrace *El Árbol* as a guiding symbol is that it draws attention to core strengths of NLERAP that are deeply embedded in our sense of who we are as a collective. The rooted tree is a reminder that we collectively possess and honor our community's cultural wealth (Yosso, 2005, 2006); our funds of knowledge (González et al., 1993; Moll & Greenberg, 1990); the sacrifices, knowledge, spirituality, wisdom of our ancestors; and our connection to community (Facio & Lara, 2014; Pizarro, 1998). At the same time, *El Árbol* signals that transformational change, particularly regarding educators' identities, does not happen quickly or by command (Clark & Flores, 2001; Galindo, 1996). The old growth represents our histories of struggle and survival that provide seeds of experience and wisdom that can inform political action today. As opposed to a political orientation that stresses careerism and résumé building, the generational consciousness that we seek is one that is individually and collectively guided by a social justice ethic that is responsive to the deepening inequalities and inequities in our society and their implications for future generations.

Perhaps the time for generational thinking could not be more ripe, given that the number of close to "90 million [Latina and Latino] teens to 30-somethings is even more formidable than the aging baby-boom generation" (El Nasser, 2014, n.p.). Further noteworthy as an opportunity is the unprecedented number of college-going Latinos in the United States in recent years (Fry & López, 2012). Members of this generation stand to benefit from an exploration into the relationship of biography and history, the personal and the social, the location of groups within the larger social structure, and the discourses that legitimate societal hierarchies so that they might derive a critical understanding of—as well as a sense of responsibility toward—unjust policies and practices in order to alleviate human suffering (Mannheim, 1923/1952; also see Pilcher [1994]).

This deeply rooted sense of history and identity extends well beyond the present and the material to include the spiritual and onto-logical (Flores, Vasquez, & Clark, 2014). We draw on ancestral knowl-edge and wisdom as well as research evidence to help us identify and challenge colonizing practices in education that reinscribe hierarchi-cal relations of power. Moreover, our collective history and shared identities as subaltern, community-engaged scholars uniquely equips us with a tangible sense of the ingredients that will contribute to the long-term sustainability of our project. This sensibility guides our de-cision to center our GYO-TEI initiatives in community-based organi-zations (CBOs), partnered with universities and schools. Moreover, these CBOs have a track record of working in and with the Latino community, specifically in the area of education. Our community-based organizations and partnering educational institutions currently consist of the following:

- El Puente (http://elpuente.us/), involving students from El Puente High School's Project for Peace and Justice in partnership with Brooklyn College, New York
- The Puerto Rican Community Center (http://prcc-chgo.org/), involving students from Roberto Clemente High School, partnering with Northeastern Illinois University (note that our work at Northeastern Illinois builds on the university's existing GYO initiative, described in Skinner, Garreton, and Schultz [2011])
- Families in Schools in Los Angeles (http://www .familiesinschools.org/) and the Sol Collective in Sacramento (http://freesolarts.wordpress.com/), California, involving students from McClatchy High School, partnering with California State University, Sacramento
- Council for the Spanish Speaking, Inc. (http://www .centrohispanomke.org/), involving students from South Division High School, partnering with the Milwaukee Area Technical College and the University of Wisconsin–Milwaukee
- The League of United Latin American Citizens (LULAC), LULAC's National Educational Service Centers, Inc. (http://www .lnesc.org/), and the Hispanic Institute for Progress, Inc. (HIPI),

as well as involving students from Sunset High School in Dallas, Texas, partnering with the University of North Texas, Dallas

NLERAP'S POLITICAL GENEALOGY

Although NLERAP was officially founded approximately 15 years ago, its roots date back much earlier, to 1983, when it existed as a collective within the Inter-University Program for Latino Research (IUPLR, 2015). The historical lineage of IUPLR (2015) can be traced to the institutionalization of Mexican American/Chicano and Puerto Rican/Boricua Study Centers in universities throughout the nation. Our centers have a proud genealogy as an outgrowth of the civil rights movement and of organizations such as the Raza Unida Party, the Mexican American Legal Defense and Education Fund, the Puerto Rican Legal Defense and Education Fund, the ASPIRA Association, the G.I. Forum, LULAC, the National Association for the Advancement of Colored People, and the National Council of la Raza. Tracing our genealogy back even further, we can invoke tribal governance structures and long roots of community organizing that simultaneously reveal the continuity of movement struggles through activist generational cohorts (Garcia, 1991; Urrieta, 2009; Zamora, 2008) and extend our reach as an organization, by centuries, to the indigenous people of this continent (Cintli Rodriguez, 2014; Zamora, 2014).

The act of building institutions such as NLERAP, and now our GYO-TEI initiative, reflects in part a reawakening to the wisdom of our ancestors, and in part a mounting concern over harmful public policies, narrow public discourses, scripted curricula, market-based reforms, and monetized ways of knowing and being in the world. These contemporary trends not only threaten our civil and human rights, but also endanger our access to the very wisdom and knowledge from which all people can derive maximum benefit. The unrelenting attacks on bilingual education and ethnic studies, along with the unabated rhetorical and actual right-wing attacks against our immigrant community, speak in great part to our collective histories and experiences as subalterns in the United States (see Sleeter [2011] for a comprehensive review on the academic and social value of ethnic studies). In addition, they call upon us to reach deeply into our histories and identities of struggle in order to derive a sense of direction for the present and the future, both for ourselves and for the generations that follow.

AT THE GRASSROOTS: COMMUNITY ACTORS
AND UNIVERSITY SUPPORTERS

Rather than the more typical configuration of being university centered and community linked, NLERAP's GYO-TEI initiative is community based and university connected. With this reversal, we seek to preempt an ironic characteristic of reforms in which the community is more of an afterthought than a valued partner. Succinctly, efforts to transform education in a sustaining way are jeopardized when they lack a community on the ground that understands and supports this transformation. In the best of worlds, the community is much more than a supporting actor: It is a founding partner and respected co-equal that guides the overall initiative as the primary stakeholder of the reform (Simmons, 2011; Tyack & Cuban, 1995; Valenzuela & López, 2014).

To this end, in addition to a regional director (or codirectors recruited from within the community), each of our five GYO-TEI sites has a NLERAP advisory board. Advisory boards are variously comprised of university faculty, researchers, students, parents, community advocates, and leaders. Site directors regularly convene their respective advisory boards in order to jointly work out the roles and responsibilities of the various members of the partnership and to plan and implement specific aspects of the initiative. Primary partners typically consist of CBO, community, school district, and university personnel who collectively share ownership of the GYO-TEI initiative. Indeed, the most important work of our initiative is carried out by all of these partners located on the ground at their respective sites.

In short, NLERAP helps to both legitimate and motivate grassroots initiatives that involve participating schools or feeder patterns, along with participating universities, at each of our sites. Because the GYO-TEI initiative is not simply about supporting or supplementing the work of traditional public schools, but is also about promoting systemic change in how teacher preparation is administered at the higher education level, our public universities must always be part of the equation. Through our collective research-based knowledge, our written histories, and the voices of our communities working in partnership with university faculty and leadership, our GYO-TEI effort opens up the "white box" of teacher preparation in higher education (Urrieta, 2009). Our goal here is to thoughtfully reorient power relationships in order to harvest a new generation of organic, secondary school teachers who are authentically caring, culturally competent, social justice oriented, and well equipped to teach a diverse Latino demographic, as well as other students of color and/or language-minority groups.

Our grassroots regional advisory board structure and leadership work to nurture and leverage community strength so that our communities can work with and through departments and colleges and universities, on the one hand, and with and through school and district administration bureaucracies, on the other, to create more impact than any of us could achieve as individuals. Mark Warren and Karen Mapp (2011) refer to this as "relational power" and aptly note the challenges in developing an agenda for social change led by institutions that prefer not to share power or, relatedly, ones that are already in pursuit of their own independent, self-defined reform agendas. Similarly, Wilson (2008) calls for "relationality" in the research process from an indigenous perspective whenever we, as researchers, are engaged in projects that seek to better others' lives.

To these useful insights of relational power and relationality we add another, namely, that large institutions such as universities or school districts are often calcified by the demands associated with carrying out their missions. This can lead to situations in which diverse constituencies may be working hard, but may be working either at cross-purposes or without directionality, lacking in vision, mission, and purpose.

AT THE GRASSTOPS: A NATIONAL CONSORTIUM, A NATIONAL OFFICE, AND A NONPROFIT

Our grasstops approach has three components: the NLERAP Council (our "brain trust"); the NLERAP national office, located at the University of Texas at Austin; and NLERAP, Inc., a legally constituted, national nonprofit that focuses on fundraising. We discuss each of these components separately in the following sections (see NLERAP.org to learn about our national organizational structure and membership).

The Brain Trust

The NLERAP Council (hereafter also referred to as the Council) comprises a national network of educators, community activists, university scholars, and other educational stakeholders that collectively represent at least 400 years of accumulated knowledge, wisdom, and experience—thus, a "brain trust." Over a decade ago, under the leadership of NLERAP cofounders Pedro Pedraza and Melissa Rivera, the Council developed organically out of consensus-building dialogues with Latino community members and stakeholders. These conversations were held over the 2-year period from 2000 to 2002 in eight different cities in states across the country, and in Puerto Rico. Discussions pertained to the educational crisis confronting our communities, with a deliberate focus on developing an actionable research agenda to address this crisis.

After a series of regional meetings, the Council developed and published a research agenda (National Latino Education Research Agenda Project, 2003). It outlines four areas of concern that were identified during the community dialogues:

1. The disappearance of the arts from our public school curricula;
2. The negative impact of high-stakes testing;
3. The lack of sociocultural and sociopolitical perspectives in classroom learning; and
4. The shortcomings of the (overwhelmingly non-Latino) teachers instructing Latino students (these teachers were viewed as showing a systemic lack of sensitivity toward Latino children and youth and providing them with an ineffective education).

Bilingual education emerged as a fifth topic of importance during the dialogues. However, because various state and national entities were already addressing that concern, the Council decided to concentrate NLERAP's efforts on the other four topics.

In addition to the research agenda, the community dialogues project also resulted in the publication of an academic volume that outlines a collaborative, community-based approach to the investigation of schooling for Latinos (Pedraza & Rivera, 2005). The book notes another concern expressed during the community conversations: Research-based knowledge does not inform policy debates in a timely way. We ascertained not only the necessity of a much quicker timeline responsive to the needs of our communities, but also a more engaged approach to policy that we now term, "engaged policy" (Foley & Valenzuela, 2005; López, Valenzuela, & Garcia, 2011; Valenzuela & López, 2014). An early response to our communities' concerns included a press briefing on Capitol Hill on March 15, 2002, at which several in our group addressed the harmful effects of high-stakes testing on Latino youth, as well as student retention, based on evidence gathered from our respective sites (e.g., Valenzuela, 2005).

All of this prior work culminated, and found expression, in a decision made by the NLERAP Council on January 31, 2009, to pursue what we now term the GYO-TEI initiative. That initiative articulates our vision to grow a critical mass of critically conscious Latina and Latino educators who would emanate from their own communities and then return to them as "NLERAP teachers" of Latino and other youth of color. For now, we are focusing specifically on developing future high school teachers of Latino youth. In the future, we envision growing our own elementary and middle school teachers of Latino and other youth of color, as well as our own administrators, board members, and the like—all of whom have a stake in the prosperity of their own communities. Our efforts are thus simultaneously anchored in community development and school district efforts (Simmons, 2011), even as we forge partnerships with higher education institutions in order to carry out our GYO-TEI vision.

The GYO-TEI initiative was the brainchild of renowned scholar and NLERAP founding member Dr. Sonia Nieto. During the day-long meeting of the Council and the Ford Foundation held on January 30, 2009, NLERAP Council member Dr. Ana Maria Villegas presented national-level data on the disproportionate number of Latina and Latino teachers relative to our community's growing majority of school-aged children and youth. Following that presentation, Dr. Nieto suggested that NLERAP should respond to the community's concern regarding the quality of the majority of teachers currently instructing Latino students. She proposed the establishment of teacher preparation institutes where we would bring together our collective "best practices" to begin transforming university-based teacher preparation programs across the country while simultaneously increasing the representation of critically conscious Latina and Latino teachers. This idea presaged not only the creation of the pathways into teaching upon which our aforementioned partnerships are predicated, but also the development of curricula—of which this handbook is a foundational part.

The National Office

Since 2008, NLERAP's national office has been located within Dr. Angela Valenzuela's administrative portfolio as director of the Texas Center for Education Policy (TCEP) at the University of Texas at

Austin. From 2008 to 2013, Dr. Valenzuela worked with former Associate Director Dr. Patricia D. López. Prior to this, NLERAP was housed at the City University of New York Hunter College under the leadership of Pedro Pedraza, who codirected NLERAP with Melissa Rivera from 2000 until his retirement in 2008. During a transition phase from 2007 to 2008, the name of the organization also changed from the National Latino/a Education Research Agenda Project to its current name. This change signaled a stronger focus on policy for the organization, as well as its new home in TCEP (Valenzuela & López, 2015).

The main tasks of this administrative portfolio are to cultivate the GYO-TEI initiative; to oversee the research activities of NLERAP's national committees and the work of the organization's affiliated scholars, generally; and to respond to communities' requests for NLERAP's involvement in research, community dialogues, policy debates, and policymaking across our sites and at the federal level. Rather than enduring the long wait for research results to provide guidance on the effectiveness of reform efforts aimed at improving the schooling of Latinos, our brain trust of scholars, leaders, and community advocates seeks to "put their work to work" by facilitating the flow of research-based knowledge and information to stakeholders throughout our sites so that this information may readily serve our communities' purposes (see López and Valenzuela [2014] for elaboration). As this handbook illustrates, we already know much about what needs to be done in order to improve, and indeed transform, the quality of Latino students' schooling experiences. The GYO-TEI initiative—working in tandem with NLERAP's brain trust—makes this knowledge actionable.

The Nonprofit

The third component of our grasstops approach is NLERAP, Inc., a 501(c)3 nonprofit that serves as the fundraising and sustainability arm of our national office. NLERAP, Inc. is located in Dallas. The nonprofit has a board of trustees, including businesspeople, whose participation allows us to tap the corporate sector and other private sources of funding and philanthropy. The goal of the nonprofit is to ensure that our GYO-TEI sites are self-sustaining, and that our CBO sits at the helm of progressive change, far into the future, as well. We exercised care in making the decision to partner with business, seeking out a particular segment of this community with deep and abiding commitments to civil rights and public education.

Because of today's neoliberal context, discussions on charter schools, a particularly contentious topic among us, are unavoidable. We have discussed numerous times whether to include them in our partnership framework because many such schools exist primarily because of the failures of public education in our communities. Thus, while acknowledging the good reasons for many charter schools to exist—particularly public or community-based charters—our preference to date has been to avoid sending mixed signals by bringing them under NLERAP's umbrella, particularly when community–school–university partnerships are an excellent alternative. These partnerships are optimally contractual or consist of memoranda of understanding.

What unites us is the inspiration drawn from our sites that unearth and reveal the continuing potential of public education in concert with community to serve democratic, social justice ends (Glass & Wong, 2003). The fact of a very large and growing Latino student demographic in our public school system, relative to other groups in the K–12 public sector, is also compelling. Data analysis by Murphey, Guzman, and Torres (2014; also see Krogstad, 2014; Fry, 2008; Fry & Gonzáles, 2008) observes a high rate of Latino demographic growth over the past several decades. The number of states in which at least one in five public school kindergartners is Latino has increased. Currently, there are 17 states in which Latino children comprise at least 20% of the public school kindergarten population. In contrast, in 2000, only eight states had such a composition (Krogstad, 2014).

Although the symbol of *El Árbol* certainly speaks to the very rich, deep, and conflicted histories and legacies that connect us to one another, at its core, *El Árbol* represents shared and unifying values, principles, and stories that are in turn grounded in a social justice vision and shared identification with a continent that dates our collective presence to 7,000 years ago (Cintli Rodriguez, 2014; Four Arrows et al., 2013)—and even earlier to 13,500 B.C. if considering its first inhabitants (Dixon, 2000). The sense of rootedness that this indigenous way of knowing provides is the antidote to 500 years of dehumanization and colonization (Valenzuela, 2010). It helps us to withstand the emotional, psychic, and spiritual freight of toxic, racialized political and policy agendas that construct our Mexican, Latino, and immigrant students and their families as "aliens," "foreigners," and "illegals," on the one hand, and their language use and preferences as a "problem," "barrier," or "impediment," on the other. Through the Mayan concept of *Panche Be* to which we subscribe, Cintli Rodriguez (2014) captures well these combined notions of rootedness, identity, story, and values that have the potential to unite all of humanity:

> Panche Be is Buscar la Raíz de la Verdad or To Seek the Root of the Truth (or To Find the Truth in the Root[s]). This concept is not simply about the search for the truth, or even about teaching students to be critical thinkers, but about the pursuit of peace, dignity, and justice. (p. 176)

NURTURING THE NEXT GENERATION OF LATINA AND LATINO GROW YOUR OWN TEACHERS

This section lays out the background assumptions and critical multicultural education framework that guides the preparation of teachers in the context of our GYO-TEI initiative. It explicates, as well, the signature courses and PAR approach to our method.

Background Assumptions

First, U.S. Latinos are such a diverse group that no entity can possibly claim, with any amount of exactitude, that there is one best method for teaching this demographic effectively. Latinos/as can be of any race, and they differ by class, language, dialect, linguistic fluency in English and Spanish, region of the country from which they emanate, documentation status and generational status in the United States, and preferred self-referents that reflect this enormous diversity—for example, Boricua, Puerto Rican, Nuyorican, Mexican, Mexican American, Chicano/a, Tejano/a, Mexicano/a, Latino/a, Native American, Indigenous, Dominican, Salvadorian, Cubano/a, and so on. Second, being a Latina or Latino preservice or inservice teacher does not in itself make one a good teacher. Third, being a preservice or inservice teacher who speaks Spanish does not in itself make one a good teacher. Fourth, even when preservice or inservice GYO teachers emanate from a particular community within one of our partnerships, we do not assume that their schooling experiences, either as teachers or students, have provided them with the kind of "critical multicultural capital" that this handbook facilitates. Drawing on Bryson (1996), who in turn drew on Bourdieu (1977), and Achinstein and Ogawa (2011), we marshal the term *critical multicultural capital* to describe schooling contexts that support the development of cultural knowledge and resources in order to respond affirmatively and equitably to culturally and linguistically diverse cultural contexts. We add the term *critical* in order to preserve our emphasis on the transformative educator whom we seek to cultivate in the context of our GYO-TEI initiative.

Researchers find, for example, that in schools where fellow teachers have limited experience and minimal preparation, opportunities for both learning and quality mentorship for novice teachers of color are scarcely available (Achinstein & Ogawa, 2011; Quiocho & Rios, 2000). Assimilationist approaches to schooling in such contexts prevail, meaning that linguistically and culturally responsive teaching practices and curricula are largely absent (Valenzuela, 1999). Moreover, minority[1] preservice teachers from contexts like these may have unknowingly internalized the negative, often stereotypic, views of their own racial and ethnic groups, making it difficult for them to fully understand how institutions systematically contribute to the maintenance and reproduction of inequality in schools and society.

With these assumptions, we make a general point that critically conscious educators are developed and nurtured rather than automatically predisposed by virtue of a shared race or ethnicity. Accordingly, a final grounding assumption that guides the preparation of future teachers of Latino youth is that the multicultural critical framework that characterizes this handbook is necessary for *all* students in a democracy, as cogently expressed by Nieto (1996):

> Multicultural education is a process of comprehensive school reform and basic education for all students. It challenges and rejects racism and other forms of discrimination in schools and society and accepts and affirms the pluralism (ethnic, racial, linguistic, religious, economic, and gender, among others) that students, their communities, and teachers represent. Multicultural education permeates the curriculum and instructional strategies used in schools, as well as the interactions among teachers, students and parents, and the very way that schools conceptualize the nature of teaching and learning. Because it uses critical pedagogy as its underlying philosophy and focuses on knowledge, reflection, and action (praxis) as the basis for social change, multicultural education furthers the democratic principles of social justice. (p. 307)

According to Nieto (1996), the seven basic characteristics of multicultural education in this definition are as follows:

Multicultural education is *antiracist education*.
Multicultural education is *basic education*.
Multicultural education is *important for* all *students*.
Multicultural education is *pervasive*.
Multicultural education is *education for social justice*.
Multicultural education is a *process*.
Multicultural education is *critical pedagogy*. (p. 308)

Accordingly, what we offer is a curriculum that moves youth of color from the margins to the center—philosophically, morally, intellectually, and politically. We admittedly set a high bar, but we also provide a framework for instruction and action that makes up a large part of this handbook. And this is a framework that we ourselves either abide—or plan to abide—by at each of our sites.

Signature Courses

This handbook provides content for the two signature courses that—based on prior discussions and agreements—are being, or will be, taught at each GYO-TEI site. Although they have various course names and titles across our sites, these courses focus on sociocultural and sociopolitical awareness, respectively. Many universities already incorporate sociocultural courses that teach preservice teachers about language, culture, difference, power, language acquisition, language learning, bilingual education models, and the like. Less frequently taught are courses that offer sociopolitical content that addresses policy, politics, social movements, legislative and judicial battles, legal precedents, laws, civil rights history, critical race theory, and the like.

Participatory Action Research

To these courses, we further recommend that you consider incorporating a community-based, participatory action research (PAR) approach to understanding educational and societal issues in order to help solve real-world problems that students and their families and communities face in their lives. In contrast to what is commonly referred to as service learning, PAR involves research in partnership with communities of the kind that NLERAP offers. This handbook provides a framework, exercises, and case study examples that will certainly move most university faculty and inservice teachers out of their comfort zones in order to equip them to develop PAR projects in their secondary classrooms.

Each site will determine how the material contained within this handbook will inform the syllabi developed for those specific courses. Philosophically, however, we call for community-centered partnerships with universities that are invested in adopting this curriculum so that our classrooms and schools can become relevant to the lived experiences and social struggles of the communities from which our teacher recruits are drawn. Efficacy with PAR engenders the kinds of orientations and dispositions that enable our GYO recruits to return to their communities as transformational agents of change, possessing enhanced capacities to respond to the needs, wishes, and concerns of their communities (Ayala et al., 2012; Cammarota & Fine, 2008). There are no shortcuts. In order for them to be able to become change agents, we ourselves as university faculty must model the very changes that we seek.

WHY GROWING OUR OWN TEACHERS MAKES SENSE: WHAT THE RESEARCH SAYS

Our GYO-TEI initiative draws from a wealth of research that reveals the impact that quality teachers have on the learning and education of all youth. In addition, we put into practice the idea of multiple pathways that call for partnering public schools with institutions of higher education. The goal is to provide opportunities for students—in this case, future teachers—to acquire a combination of academic and real-world preparation that will facilitate their successful entry into teaching careers (Oakes & Saunders, 2008).

Research studies provide the following insights about the potential benefits to students of high-quality, Latina or Latino teachers: First, high-quality teachers are the single most determining school-based factor that correlates with student achievement, graduation rates, and college eligibility among Latino youth (Center for Research on Education, Diversity & Excellence [CREDE], 2001; Darling-Hammond, 2003; Garcia, 2001). Thus, having a highly skilled classroom teacher who fosters academic rigor, high expectations, and collaborative relationships among peers of diverse backgrounds increases the possibility that students will be presented with learning opportunities of a higher order that are also imaginative, engaging, and likely to promote advanced levels of all forms of literacy alongside the development of social skills essential for success in career, community, and life.

Second, a demand exists. Latino students—whose growth rate exceeds that of any other student subpopulation in our nation's public schools (Fry, 2008; Fry & Gonzáles, 2008; National Clearinghouse for English Language Acquisition, 2007)—are systematically deprived of access to quality instruction. They are more likely to attend poor, segregated, and under-resourced schools where not only is quality instruction a scarce commodity (Darling-Hammond, 2000, 2003; Nieto, 2005), but a lack of Latino teachers translates into "an immense disequilibrium between the students' cultures and that of the school" (Gutierrez-Gomez, 2007, p. 334).

Third, Latina and Latino teachers are more likely to teach in hard-to-staff schools (Villegas, 2007; Villegas & Clewell, 1998) and to have higher retention rates than their White peers in these same schools (Achinstein, Ogawa, Sexton, & Freitas, 2010; Kirby, Berends, & Naftel, 1999; Villegas, 2009). Consequently, a significant positive return on investment in this emergent workforce may be expected (also see Villegas and Lucas [2001, 2002]).

Fourth, an emerging body of research on racial congruence finds that relative to their Anglo counterparts, the students of Latino teachers register higher test scores, as well as better attendance, retention, and college-going rates for students of color (Clewell, Puma, & McKay, 2005; Dee, 2004; Egalite, Kisida, & Winters, 2015; Villegas & Irvine, 2010). A statistical analysis by Meier, Wrinkle, and Polinard (1999) additionally found that the test scores of Anglo students also benefit from a large presence of teachers of color.

In a second reanalysis of their data, Meier, Eller, Wrinkle, and Polinard (2001) successfully rebut criticisms by Nielsen and Wolf (1999) of the aforementioned study with even more evidence that at a particular threshold, or "critical mass," Latino (as well as African American) teachers improve Anglo student achievement for reasons that, they maintain, are lodged in the theoretical framework of representative bureaucracy (Meier & Smith, 1994). Specifically, when a critical mass of Latino teachers is present, these teachers have more voice and can advocate better for their students, families, and communities. Their presence in large numbers is associated with the election of Latino school board members who can advocate for their interests and provide political support for their opinions and demands. This pool of teachers also serves as the base of those who will later become

Latino administrators, who, after achieving a critical mass, will foster ever-greater representation among both the teaching and adminis-trative ranks, as well. Policies and practices such as tracking, ability grouping, disciplinary actions, and adversely labeling youth are easier to change when administrators' size as a group is ample, and as a con-sequence, more influential (Meier & Stewart, 1991).

Fifth, Latino teachers' knowledge of their students' cultures and languages is helpful to the development of constructive relationships between themselves and their students, as well as with students' parents (Bartlett & Garcia, 2011; Espinoza-Herold, 2003; Gutierrez-Gomez, 2007). Greater openness for all parties is arguably helpful when all speak the same language and otherwise share similar experi-ences and cultural frames of reference.

To be sure, learning from a curriculum that is power-evasive and subtractive of students' ethnicities, languages, and community-based identities is suboptimal and colonizing (Valenzuela, 1999). What is needed instead is a curricular and instructional approach that is as-set based, valorizes the cultural wealth of our students' communi-ties (Yosso, 2005, 2006), and creates pathways into higher education and careers that are not generally available to low-income students of color (Stanton-Salazar, 1997). Our investments in growing this GYO-TEI initiative must therefore align faithfully to a clear vision, an artic-ulated mission, and guiding principles, together with an infrastructure grounded in community-based partnerships, in order to ensure long-term sustainability (see Appendix A, "NLERAP's Guiding Principles and Expected Teacher Competencies").

Regarding the concept of multiple pathways, although we strive to encourage college-eligible youth to consider careers in teaching, we are also amenable to other routes, including paraprofessional and postbaccalaureate pathways. In all instances, we seek GYO teachers who express an interest in returning either to their neighborhoods or communities of origin—or those similar to ones that they are from—to pursue teaching careers.

In summary, NLERAP's GYO Latina or Latino teacher strategy is an extended, multiyear commitment to invigorate under-resourced schools and communities with an ongoing infusion of human, mate-rial, and intellectual resources. Pragmatically speaking, our aim is to ad-dress the teacher shortage and teacher preparation crises in our nation, particularly with respect to future teachers of culturally diverse class-rooms; address multilevel (local, state, and national) policies that either positively address or perpetuate the undersupply of quality teachers across the initiative's sites and beyond; and grow our own critically conscious teachers for future students of Latino and other minority youth. However, we also aspire to reinvigorate the deeply rooted structure of our democratic traditions, cultural values, and civic ideals in order to sow the seeds of renewal and transformation that we as a collective, and our planet as a whole, desperately need, one teacher at a time.

Bienvenidos!/Welcome! This has been an exciting journey for us, and we hope that this will be an exciting journey for you, as well.

NOTE

1. This volume uses the phrases *teachers of color* and *minority teachers* interchangeably. The sociological term *minority* is not a numerical term, but rather references the historical fact that Latinos/as are a cultural, political, social, and economic minority. It therefore refers to power and not numbers. South Africa is a good example of how being a member of a demographic majority does not translate into cultural, political, social, and economic power that reflects this (Feagin & Feagin, 2011).

CHAPTER 2

Teacher Capacities for Latino and Latina Youth

Carmen I. Mercado

Insufficient attention has been paid to developing teacher capacities for teaching students from marginalized communities. Concerns over low achievement levels in mathematics and science have propelled educators in these fields to take the lead in determining teacher capacities, but these assessments typically use a traditional "neutral" framework in which the role of race or power is left unexamined (Grant, 2008). However, Latino students, shaped by experiences of marginalization associated with social and economic inequalities, come to school with both developmental risks and benefits that affect school performance. Teachers must understand these risks and benefits in order to support access to intellectually challenging curricular content, particularly in science, mathematics, and technology (Darder, 1997; Garcia Coll & Szalacha, 1996).

The problem is that well-intentioned, but poorly conceived policies and practices place an imbalanced emphasis on achievement that is typically narrowly defined in terms of standardized test scores. Consequently, the press for accountability resulting from the No Child Left Behind Act (NCLB) has reduced the curriculum to the teaching of reading and mathematics, and the undertaking of drills and other exercises aimed at improving test scores. In the shift to fragmented and rote forms of teaching and learning (e.g., Valenzuela, 2005), the significance of sociocultural influences on the process of schooling have been neglected. At a minimum, teachers must be prepared with understandings and practices that will help them integrate issues of identity, language difference, culture, and power into the core curriculum (i.e., English language arts, mathematics, social studies, and science), drawing on students' assets and the cultural wealth of their communities (Yosso, 2005).

The purpose of this chapter is to provide a rationale that answers the question, "What individual and collective capacities (i.e., professional knowledge, skills, and dispositions) do new teachers need to promote equitable access to knowledge, resources, and opportunities for Latinos attending under-resourced schools?" The capacities explored in this chapter are in keeping with a vision of education that seeks to develop students' full potential as human beings who are responsible for making ours a better world, and who are prepared for work and for life. This is the vision that shapes the work of the National Latino/a Education Research and Policy Project (NLERAP); also see Nieto, Rivera, Quiñones, and Irizarry (2012) for an earlier articulation of this vision. Our organization further exemplifies the sustainable community-centered reform that the Annenberg Institute for School Reform has found to be successful (Simmons, 2011).

UNDERSTANDING TEACHER CAPACITIES

Over the many decades of debates about what makes a good teacher and what capacities teachers need to be good teachers (Grant, 2008), definitions of teacher capacities have changed. These changes are a response to larger social shifts and new social needs, and they usually reflect consensus among influential educational scholars and leaders who have as their mission the improvement of teacher preparation (e.g., see Interstate Teacher Assessment and Support Consortium [InTASC], 2010; National Council for Accreditation of Teacher Education [NCATE], 2008). However, community groups also shape the knowledge, skills, and dispositions of teachers, as Mercado and Reyes (2010) describe in their historical analysis of community activism in education. This analysis provides two examples that highlight the power of local communities in shaping teacher capacities to meet local needs. In the first example (see Apple, 1996), coalitions of community groups contested the teaching of evolution and succeeded in changing the public school curriculum to include the study of creationism, a subject consonant with their beliefs. Through their advocacy, community groups who represented a minority view were able to redefine the knowledge teachers should have to teach effectively in that community.

In the second example (see Mercado, 2012), the Puerto Rican community in New York City used the legal system to secure Spanish/English bilingual instruction for U.S. citizens who were denied access to instruction in a language they understood. Working at the height of the civil rights movement, coalitions of diverse groups secured bilingual instruction, a new bilingual teaching certificate, and programs to recruit and prepare bilingual teachers. However, because education is political, when shifts in power occur, the number of teachers of color who are hired also fluctuates with changes in recruitment and credentialing practices and curriculum standardization, as was dramatically evident after the election of President Reagan in 1980 (Mercado, 2012).

Contrary to popular opinion, researchers cannot uniformly predict teacher quality across demographic groups on the basis of their scores on licensure exams (Goldhaber & Hansen, 2008). Over the past decade, teachers with strong academic credentials recruited through policies derived from NCLB have made only modest improvement in student achievement in the poorest schools (Boyd, Grossman, Lankford, Loeb, & Wyckoff, 2005). This is particularly true in the many underachieving (or ineffective) schools serving Latino communities. Teacher quality is context specific, and teachers who are highly effective in one setting are not necessarily so in another (Dall'Alba & Sandberg, 2006; Goldhaber & Anthony, 2003). At a minimum, teachers must have the capacity to build positive relationships with students, to understand and value local community funds of knowledge and use these to organize rigorous learning activities, and engage in ongoing inquiry to assess participation and learning (González et al., 1993; Moll & Greenberg, 1990).

However, as noted in the previous chapter, Latino and African American teachers are underrepresented in the workforce. In 2011, only 2% of teachers were African American men, and only 2% were Latino men (Duncan, 2010, p. 13). Overall, in 2011–2012, 24% of all public school teachers were male (National Center for Education Statistics, 2014). I am not suggesting that a teacher's race/ethnicity and capacity automatically correlate, although Nieto's (2005) research shows that minority race/ethnicity can help teachers relate to their students and thus benefit children and youth from marginalized Latino communities.

Thus, Latino students, who now constitute the public school majority, will have fewer future possibilities for mobility if their teachers lack the capacities to make challenging curricular content accessible to them, which is arguably a key factor in school success. Secretary of Education Arne Duncan (2010) acknowledges that students benefit when they learn from teachers with whom they can identify and from those who can be strong role models. In response to the "disappearance of Black and Latino/a teachers" in New York City public schools, the Delegate Assembly of the United Federation of Teachers (UFT) approved a resolution that advocates the hiring of teachers of color on the grounds that these teachers use sound pedagogy, advance labor solidarity, and move us closer to the ideals of a democratic society (United Federation of Teachers Committee on Social and Economic Justice, 2008).

Gloria Ladson-Billings, a former president of the American Education Research Association (AERA), agrees that the purpose of diversifying the teaching workforce is to experience a more accurate picture of what it means to live and work in a multicultural and democratic society to the benefit of all children (Ladson-Billings, 2005). There is consensus among scholars and leaders from professional and community groups that, however complementary to existing norms, the characteristics of competent Latina and Latino teachers are distinct from those of other sectors of the U.S. teaching workforce in that they develop unique assets through life experiences as minorities in U.S. society. These assets—which might include, for example, emergent bilingualism and biliteracy, knowledge of Latino communities, and an orientation toward being of service to community—provide a strong foundation for teaching. Further, there is evidence that teachers with these qualities have a positive influence on Latino students' school success and aspirations for the future (Huerta & Brittain, 2010; Oliva & Staudt, 2003; Quiocho & Rios, 2000; Reyes & Halcón, 2001).

Making comparisons across ethnolinguistic categories may be of questionable value, however, given the relatively small percentages of Latina and Latino teachers in a teaching workforce that is overwhelmingly composed of non-Hispanic Whites. A more reasonable course of action is suggested by the UFT Delegate Assembly, which offers this advice: Identify corrective measures, initiatives, and changes in policy that increase the percentage of teachers of color in New York City public schools so that these may serve as guideposts for positive action vis-à-vis their underrepresentation in the teacher workforce. I would extend this imperative to *all* public school districts throughout the nation.

COMMUNITY-ORIENTED TEACHING CAPACITIES

The identification of capacities needed to unleash the potential that resides in Latino communities is a first step in developing the community-oriented teacher preparation that NLERAP proposes. There is a new body of scholarship rooted in the wisdom, values, and life experiences of Latinos that emerges from the work of Latino and African American scholars (see, e.g., Antrop-González & De Jesús, 2006; Brittain, 2009; Dillard, 2000; Dillard, Abdur-Rashid, & Tyson, 2006; Faltis, Arias, & Ramírez-Marín, 2010; Galván, 2010; hooks, 1994; Huerta & Brittain, 2010; Mercado & Brochin-Ceballos, 2011; Valenzuela, 1999; Villenas, 2009). Influential scholarship on teaching also informs this effort (e.g., Darling-Hammond & Bransford, 2005; Haberman, 2005; Schulman, 2005).

Capacities derived from these two sources of scholarship are combined and organized using the framework that guides the professional preparation of teachers (see InTASC, 2010; NCATE, 2008). Although it is important to recognize this framework because it is presently used to determine whether state-certified teacher preparation programs meet quality criteria, it should be noted that the usefulness of the framework is limited by its narrow focus on the capacities of individual teachers, as Plecki and Loeb (2004) have suggested. At best, the framework serves as a starting point for a more comprehensive exploration of how to better serve Latino students in traditional public school contexts that include attention to the quality of support teachers receive in the workplace. The framework calls attention to the following three specific areas and the practices or "indicators" associated with each of these areas (NCATE, 2008):

- What teachers know—or knowledge
- What teachers should be able to do—or skills
- What teachers believe and are willing to do—or dispositions

It is important to acknowledge that dispositions—or habits of thinking and action about teaching children (Darling-Hammond & Bransford, 2005, p. 387)—are the engines that drive capacities related to knowledge and skills, and these are especially significant when it comes to working with children and youth from marginalized communities. Hence, the order of the following discussion does not imply any order of importance. Further, organizing the capacities needed to teach Latino students within this framework serves to illustrate how it may be adapted to be locally relevant, thus allowing for both constancy and change in teacher preparation. The discussion also serves to demonstrate how categories of competencies interact and influence one another.

Knowledge

That teachers need to have a deep knowledge or understanding of their subject, and how to make it accessible to learners, is without question. In principle, deep knowledge of subject matter enables teachers to exercise greater flexibility in adapting instruction to learner differences; however, in practice, the emphasis on subject-matter specialization has sometimes obscured other important facets of this knowledge, particularly knowledge with implications for teaching in marginalized Latino communities. Darling-Hammond and Bransford (2005) identify three areas of knowledge that are important in the preparation of teachers:

1. Knowledge of learners and how learners develop
2. Subject-matter content and skills that relate to purposes sought
3. Teaching content to specific groups of learners

Contextual Influences. As a first step, future teachers need to understand that the developmental pathways and experiences of children and youth living in segregated, low-income communities with limited access to resources (what Berliner [2009] refers to as "out-of-school influences on success") are very different from those that constitute the White, middle-class norm of development that drives mainstream teacher preparation (Weisner, 2002). Ecological models that take into account the effects that contextual influences such as poverty, racism, and discrimination have on development explain how these conditions affect minority children's growth, producing both developmental risks and benefits that shape school performance (Garcia Coll & Szalacha, 1996). Research on Latino youth (e.g., Alva, 1991) confirms that experiences of marginalization, including isolation and prejudice, in schools in low-income communities invariably rob even successful students of their self-confidence and self-worth, but these experiences do not necessarily cause irreparable harm (Sosa & Gomez, 2012). They may even act as a protective shield against later experiences with discrimination and racism. Accordingly, Garcia Coll and Szalacha (1996) explain that a segregated school environment that is inhibiting due to limited resources may simultaneously be beneficial if it equips children to both withstand prejudice and manage the societal demands imposed by the discriminatory forces of exclusion and neglect.

In a congenial context surrounded by others like themselves, children can be protected from the prejudice of the dominant culture (Alva, 1991; Sosa & Gomez, 2012). Where there is compatibility between the school and family cultural background, studies show positive effects on student achievement and school satisfaction. Stated differently, in these environments, ethnicity becomes a source of strength. Mercado (2001) and Antrop-González, Vélez, and Garrett (2003, 2005) identify protective factors that may be present in the lives of segregated, successful secondary school students. These factors include: (a) nurturance by primary caregivers such as parents, siblings, grandparents, and aunts; (b) ethnic identification; (c) critical care by teachers and other school staff; and (d) social capital accumulations acquired through religiosity and participation in school- and community-based extracurricular activities. We know from a small but fertile research base that when these efforts are successful, they also build resilience and well-being (see Antrop-González & De Jesús, 2006; Cammarota, 2004; Flores-González, 1999; Rivera & Pedraza, 2000). Teachers must understand and know how to identify and use the developmental assets of children and youth from marginalized communities, so that these assets may be marshaled in the context of an intellectually rigorous curriculum.

Lamentably, the research and knowledge base about child and youth development from an ecological perspective is the missing element in most teacher preparation programs (see Comer, 2006, p. 2). In response to this need, National Institute of Child Health and Development (NICHD) and NCATE organized a roundtable chaired by Dr. James Comer and invited a diverse group of scholars to link child development research with teacher preparation as a way of guiding teacher decisions about particular children, classes, and schools (Comer, 2006). In acknowledging the influence of sociocultural factors on learning and development, NICHD and NCATE legitimize the concerns of the NLERAP community and have therefore taken a significant step toward improving the preparation of all teachers. Teachers also need to understand that positive student–teacher relationships are integral to pedagogical practice (Antrop-González & De Jesús, 2006; Comer, 2006; Huerta & Brittain, 2010; Valenzuela, 1999).

Social and Emotional Factors. Scholars grounded in sociocultural/ecological perspectives (e.g., Bronfenbrenner, 1979; Bruner, 1996) theorize that the primary engine of human development is interpersonal relationships characterized by strong emotional attachments to those who are committed to one's well-being and development, and the presence of mutual accommodation and trust. These relationships are essential in promoting school success across the developmental continuum, as research by scholars such as Antrop-González et al. (2005), Cammarota (2004), Hidalgo (2000), and Valenzuela (1999) suggests. For example, nurturing and care in the home, combined with nurturing and care by institutional agents, helps to mitigate negative influences and provide Latino students with the tools and support they need to navigate complex systems.

Engagement in progressively complex, reciprocal activities with significant others helps develop protective factors. An unusual longitudinal study that illuminates the impact of policy on student retention and achievement was conducted by a team of scholars affiliated with New York University (Ahram, Stembridge, Fergus, & Noguera, 2011). This study documents that students of color who lack positive institutional relationships at critical points in their educational trajectories—including changes in expectations and/or in the curriculum, or consequences related to mandated testing in grades 4, 8, and 10—may exit before school completion.

In addition to knowing about and challenging the harmful impact of high-stakes tests and testing systems, teachers must anticipate and know how to provide appropriate support at these critical junctures. NICHD and NCATE (Comer, 2006) recommend that teacher education programs utilize evidence-based practices to show how emotional support and attention provided through teacher–student relationships enhance children's capacities to learn. This recommendation challenges the frequent finding of a singular focus on verbal skills in teaching traditional content. Although scholars of color have expressed both concern and interest in these aspects of teaching, they simultaneously worry that quality teacher–student relationships often get overshadowed by other matters (Antrop-González & Valenzuela, 2012; Sosa & Gomez, 2012). Understanding the importance of teacher–student relationships and learning how to build these relationships strategically takes time. Moreover, the quality of student–teacher relationships is influenced by the backgrounds and experiences of teachers themselves, many of whom lack knowledge of the local communities from which their students and their families emanate (Dai, Sindelar, Denslow, Dewey, & Rosenberg, 2005). As Nieto et al. (2012) note, this knowledge could meaningfully inform and thus benefit the instructional practices of prospective and current teachers.

Teachers also need to understand that limited school success is prompted in part by students' limited access to their sources of strength or community funds of knowledge in the learning–teaching process (Huerta & Brittain, 2010; Mercado & Brochin-Ceballos, 2011; Yosso, 2005). Sociocultural theorists and researchers argue that it is possible to shape or push development by organizing challenging activities that engage both underachieving and achieving students in intellectually rigorous work that builds emotional and intellectual connections to their social worlds. However, much of the evidence for the impact of community funds of knowledge comes from ethnographic research and testimonials by practitioner scholars of color (González, Moll, & Amanti, 2005; Mercado & Brochin-Ceballos, 2011; Mercado & Moll, 1997; Moll & Amanti, 2005). Unfortunately, this growing body of research is often not accepted as valid evidence on the grounds that it does not conform to standards that define what constitutes rigorous and reliable research in education, as emphasized in NCLB federal education policy (see Torres & Reyes, 2011, for an excellent critique of governmentality in scientific research in education).

Primacy of Student Learning. Developing the interrelated competencies of knowledge, skills, and dispositions in new teachers is complicated by the multiplicity of goals sought by teacher preparation programs, in which teaching, rather than student learning, typically is the priority (Popham, 2009). This suggests the importance of identifying critical competencies that focus on student learning in the preparation of teachers. Further, as Faltis et al. (2010) argue, there is a "knowledge gap" with respect to principles and practices geared specifically to the needs of subject-area secondary teachers working with middle and high school students who are English language learners (ELLs), a large subset of whom are Latinos. Faltis and colleagues claim that their research is a first effort to fill in this gap.

The methodological approach Faltis and his team (2010) used to identify critical competencies for secondary teachers is noteworthy. Unlike the distinctive knowledge-building approach that the NLERAP community utilizes, these researchers followed a path that aligns well with mixed-methods research. The team began by reviewing the research and pedagogical literature, employing content analysis to identify major themes—of which nine surfaced—in the teaching of ELLs. They then surveyed 40 practicing secondary school teachers from California and Arizona for consensus. That step resulted in the identification of four sets of critical competencies that those surveyed agreed new teachers must understand and practice. This mixed-methods approach offers another promising way of identifying appropriate subject-matter knowledge pertaining to a specific group of students.

The practitioners that Faltis et al. (2010) surveyed agreed that new secondary school teachers of ELLs must understand the following four critical factors:

1. Language and language learning. There was relatively strong agreement that teachers should understand the difference between social and academic language and know how learning strategies can help ELLs acquire academic content, collaborate with other teachers, and reflect on practices and ways to improve them.
2. Students' backgrounds and communities.
3. Social, cultural, and political dimensions of language.
4. Multiple assessments and language standards (there was less agreement on this factor relative to the previous three). Specifically, new teachers need to be able to diagnose and measure the challenges and strengths of the school for meeting ELLs' needs and know how to interpret state-mandated proficiency exams used to determine a student's oral and written development of English.

It is instructive that despite some differences, such as an emphasis on teaching versus learning, the findings that Faltis et al. (2010) report are strikingly similar to what NLERAP scholars describe in "Charting a New Course" (Nieto et al., 2012), as well as the research base (cited in this handbook) that has guided the creation of the signature courses that define the Grow Your Own Teacher Education Institutes (GYO-TEI) initiatives.

Skills

Skills require both head knowledge and hand knowledge, each of which takes time to develop, especially for the more complex skills required in an increasingly diverse and networked world (Ball, 2010). Influential teacher education scholars are in general agreement as to five core skills of teaching considered crucial to student learning:

- Communicating content clearly to students
- Holding students to high standards while explicitly showing students how to do complex work
- Establishing and maintaining a productive classroom climate
- Interpreting and using evidence of student performance
- Connecting effectively with students' families

In contrast, Latino and Latina scholars find that teachers of Latino students must have a broader pedagogical perspective than the current emphasis on teaching as involving the development of verbal skills and pedagogical content knowledge (Huerta & Brittain, 2010, p. 382). We see evidence of this broader perspective when teachers (a) emphasize wholeness—or the union of mind, body, and spirit (Facio & Lara, 2014; hooks, 1994); (b) stress dialogue and *convivencia* (coexistence), sharing in communal spaces of social relations (Galván, 2010, 2011); and (c) embrace a folk model of education or *educación* that accords importance to core values associated with respect and living in a way that acknowledges others' dignity (Valenzuela, 1999).

Teachers also need to make pedagogical use of everyday life (Huerta & Brittain, 2010; Ladson-Billings, 2005; Mercado & Brochin-Ceballos, 2011; Yosso, 2005). For example, they must be able to build on students' histories, stories, strengths and their families' and communities' funds of knowledge to prepare Latino students to effectively navigate institutional structures and practices so as to broaden their access to knowledge, resources, and opportunities (Moll & Gonzalez, 2004; Sosa & Gomez, 2012).

Dispositions

Dispositions are the engines that drive capacities related to knowledge and skills, and they are especially significant when it comes to working with children and youth from marginalized communities. Teaching that is oriented to the needs of local Latino communities at a time when they have to do more with less (Duncan, 2010) requires teachers who have clarity of purpose and a critical consciousness. Teachers also need to be intrinsically motivated and committed to addressing educational and economic inequalities in the context of ongoing community efforts that limit Latino students' opportunities for self-actualization. Teaching children and youth from marginalized communities comes with added responsibilities that teachers must be willing to accept, including serving as counselors, mentors, role models, and advocates. Moreover, teachers in marginalized Latino communities must be unrelenting in their efforts to build the effective sociocultural and sociopolitical knowledge that students need to sustain engagement in increasingly intellectually challenging work. It is through these experiences that students can develop their capacities for self-directed and self-regulated learning that will widen their networks of support. Further, teachers of Latino students must view teaching as a form of community service that promotes community development through equitable access to knowledge, resources, and opportunities (Nieto et al., 2012).

Haberman (2005) argues that dispositions should guide the recruitment of prospective teachers for marginalized Latino communities. Even so, there are a few examples that this vision is being enacted in the day-to day practices of teachers of color (see, e.g., Antrop-González and De Jesus [2006] in Chicago; Cammarota [2004] in Arizona; and De Jesús [2007] and Rivera, Medellín-Paz, and Pedraza [2010] in New York). Teaching, thusly defined, is therefore not entirely new. However, this approach remains largely invisible in traditional teacher preparation programs, and even when acknowledged, it has not been deliberately integrated into the praxis of teachers in marginalized communities (Grant & Agosto, 2008).

Scholarship that focuses on the ethical responsibilities of teaching in complex times complements the work of scholars of color. Lee Shulman, past president of the Carnegie Foundation for the Advancement of Teaching, coined the term "pedagogical content knowledge" (1986) to emphasize that teachers' actions must be grounded in both a deep knowledge of subject matter and how to teach that subject matter because each of these is a major influence on student learning.

Little, if any, attention has been given to understanding contextual influences that shape the learning of identifiable groups of Latino students. This may explain why Shulman also advocates for a professional preparation that focuses on developing pedagogies that link ideas, practices, and values under conditions of inherent uncertainty (Shulman, 2005). In other words, considering that available knowledge on intra-Latino student variability is limited, resulting in rather pervasive conditions of uncertainty, teachers must always have the capacity to act with sound judgment and recognize that their actions as teachers have enormous consequences for students, regardless of the level of their subject-matter expertise (Shulman, 2005). The Interstate

Teacher Assessment and Support Network (2010) adds the following: Teachers must take "ethical responsibility for student learning and use ongoing analysis and reflection to improve planning and practice" (p. 19). These educational leaders suggest that teachers must be willing to engage in labor-intensive, ongoing formative assessment to understand the consequences of well-intentioned practices if they are to modify their teaching to meet the needs of diverse learners. However, Haberman (2005), whose ideas shaped the National Teacher Corps (developed as part of the 1965 Higher Education Act) in the 1960s, has documented that effective teachers of students from marginalized communities are also persistent in finding what works to engage students even when extant practice seems to be sufficiently effective.

In sum, these respected educational leaders and scholars are in agreement that ethical teaching is an essential quality of practice in marginalized communities, as evidenced by teachers who have the capacity to: (a) act with judgment and awareness that teachers' actions always have consequences for students, (b) engage in ongoing analysis and reflection to improve planning and practice as an ethical responsibility, and (c) persist in finding what works even when what teachers are doing seems to be working. Further, these educational leaders and scholars put into question the value and utility of "best practice" research, or even the possibility of determining locally appropriate best practices under conditions of constant and intense change. Dall'Alba and Sandberg (2006) theorize that practice is intersubjectively constituted through mutual understanding enacted by professionals; therefore practice is always variable. Under these conditions, the integration of inquiry in the teaching–learning process as a professional obligation emerges as the essential best practice that is generalizable across different contexts of use.

In addition, ethical teaching involves the responsibility of keeping up with changes that affect professional practice, especially as cyber-learning becomes a dominant mode of learning. Although cyber-learning presents challenges to the uninformed, it also offers new possibilities for broadening students' learning experiences, when teachers are able to model the uses of diverse technological tools and integrate these into the curriculum in meaningful and empowering ways.

Participatory action research (PAR) is another tool that teachers may employ to assess how much youth know about, and use, technological tools and practices in informal settings outside of school, as suggested by Pea (2009). (See Appendices K ["PAR Process Hand-out"] and L ["Frequently Asked Questions about PAR"] for additional information about PAR.) Latino children and youth may have some access to portable computers, iPads, video cameras, and online learn-ing communities, but they also depend on teachers who are resource-ful and willing to learn as they teach. Latino students need access to powerful new learning technologies to become independent learners, experience school success, and participate effectively in civic life. It is important to note, however, that providing access involves more than understanding technology. It also entails recognizing issues as-sociated with technology's uses, such as the ability to evaluate the reliability and credibility of different information sources (Pea, 2009). These media have the potential to shape Latino youths' perceptions of the world, and also to alter these students themselves in ways that may not always be positive.

As a Freirean scholar, Darder (1997) maintains that teachers must prepare Latino students with critical technological literacies so that they may attain social justice goals. Kellner (2000) extends this ar-gument, claiming that new technologies require new literacies and pedagogies to ready youth to function in a high-tech economy and a rapidly changing society and polity. Under these conditions, critical literacy means understanding and resisting the homogenizing effects of a "globalization from above" that increases the power of big corpo-rations to access undereducated youth as a source of cheap labor and impose a global culture. Kellner proposes the idea of a "globalization from below" as a space for agency or social movement with the po-tential to increase access to education by groups and individuals who have been left out of the democratic process, as is true of the majority of Latinos, and suggests resisting "globalization from above" by using its institutions and instruments to attain the ideals of our democratic society.

CONCLUSION

The NLERAP community has the human capital, social networks, and determination to turn teacher preparation "upside down." Arriving at this point has taken more than a decade of collaborative, deliber-ate, and thoughtful planning. The NLERAP affiliation of networks has built and developed a strong infrastructure or foundation (see Ball,

2010) to support targeted career and workforce development via the Grow Your Own-Teacher Education Institutes. The GYO-TEIs are designed to prepare new teachers with the dispositions, understandings, and competencies that local communities deem necessary, both at entry and upon completion of teacher preparation programs, culminating in certification. With the GYO-TEI initiative under way, NLERAP is prepared to serve as a supportive intellectual community for future teachers, both locally and nationally.

This professional community also enables regional GYO-TEIs to hold themselves accountable for preparing teacher candidates with the capacities that communities deem necessary to develop Latino students' full potential as citizens of a democratic society, imbued with social justice goals and ideals, and able to work with dignity, compassion, and respect with and for all members of our society. Specifically, this community offers knowledge, tools, and resources to collaborate in the study of how identified teacher capacities impact diverse groups of Latino students, regionally and nationally.

CHAPTER 3

Teaching for Critical Consciousness
Topics, Themes, Frameworks, and Instructional Activities

Adele Arellano, José Cintrón, Barbara Flores,
and Margarita Berta-Ávila

"Everything that goes on in a classroom reflects the teacher's approach toward education. This is true whether we intend it to be so or not. Teaching is never neutral. We express our attitudes in the language we use, in the gestures and movements, in the way we maintain discipline, in our pacing of instruction, in the subject matter we cover, in the books or stories we choose to present, in the amount of time we speak and allow the students to speak, in the kinds of questions we ask, in the extent to which we involve parents and community."

—Alma Flor Ada, *A Magical Encounter* (1990)

Alma Flor Ada's observation that teaching is "never neutral" extends beyond the pre-K–12 context to include the postsecondary world of teacher preparation. Schools and colleges of education across the country select the faculty, create the curriculum, and determine access criteria and performance expectations, and everything else that prepares a future educator. Therefore, the preparation of teacher candidates is not neutral either. It never has been and never will be. Unfortunately, the prevailing and unspoken narrative in many teacher preparation programs is "don't make waves until you get tenure." New teachers replicate the same system of instruction that they received.

Likewise, decisions regarding texts, parent participation, and curriculum are passed on to another generation of educators, fueled by the ever more prescriptive and scripted curricula endorsed by states and school districts throughout the country. It should not be surprising, then, that more than 15 years into a new century, we are still attempting to figure out why our students cannot read at grade level and how best to teach so that the 5.3 million (10.6%) of the nation's schoolchildren who are English language learners have adequate access to quality academic content (Calderón, Slavin, & Sánchez, 2011).

The demographics of U.S. schools over the last few decades have experienced a burgeoning shift that has turned historically disenfranchised populations (Latinos, African Americans, and Asians/South East Asians) into the numerical majority of the U.S. school population. The change has been dramatic. In May 2012, the U.S. Census Bureau reported that the nation's minority population younger than age 1 registered at 50.4%—in contrast to 49.6% among non-Hispanic Whites. Moreover, out of 114 million minorities in 2011, this growth represented an increase from 36.1% in 2010 to 36.6% in 2011.

Conversely, minorities—including Hispanics, African Americans, Asians, and those of mixed race—reached 50.4%, representing a majority for the first time in the country's history. The report further indicates that for the first time, racial and ethnic minorities outnumber the White majority. The data further show that there are currently five majority-minority states or equivalents: Hawaii (77.1%), District of Columbia (64.7%), California (60.3%), New Mexico (59.8%), and Texas (55.2%). Recent U.S. Census (2012) data from 2011 indicate that the Latino population stands at 52 million, or approximately 57% of the nation's 2000–2010 growth rate. Adult Latinos/as now comprise one in every six Americans—and one of every four children is of Latino descent. They are now the largest minority group in the country as well as the fastest-growing subgroup, now accounting for 16.7% of the total U.S. population. Finally, along with Asians, Latinos/as constitute the youngest population base and continue to lead the nation in terms of birth rates.

Over the past few decades, much has been done to identify approaches and practices to better prepare teachers to more effectively meet the needs of culturally/linguistically different (CLD) students. In order to change practice, however, teachers need to undergo a paradigm shift. Even teacher candidates of color must continually check their belief systems, critically examine their assumptions, and guard against replicating the often unfair and inequitable conditions of the status quo educational policies and practices that result from their lack of personal knowledge or connection to their communities' histories of struggle (Bartolomé & Balderrama, 2001).

There is general agreement that teacher preparation programs must be a starting point for this shift, and yet there is little evidence of any substantial change in the curriculum and fieldwork components of most credentialing programs across the nation. In this chapter, we focus on the critical content that is often absent in teacher preparation. We believe that this content is the best foundation for preparing candidates who will help change the status quo for K–12 CLD students, in general, and for Latinos/as, specifically. We have identified overarching themes, topics, and frameworks that we believe will result in critical bilingual/multicultural teachers who are well prepared to operate within a social justice framework, and who will prepare their students to accomplish the following:

- Advocate for a social justice perspective across school, community, and political contexts.
- Use and further develop students' cultural funds of knowledge, bilingualism, and biliteracy.
- Lead students to achieve at academically high standards across the core curriculum.
- Guide students to explore issues of prejudice, discrimination, and multiple forms of oppression involving people of different races, socioeconomic classes, language varieties, abilities and disabilities, and sexual orientation.
- Engage students in naming, interrogating, and transforming deficit ideology related to culture, language, class, gender, race, and sexual orientation.
- Promote school transformation toward equity and social justice on multiple levels.

In addition, these overarching themes and curricular frameworks are related to the two signature courses that get taught at each participating Grow Your Own Teacher Education Institutes (GYO-TEI) site mentioned in Chapter 1. Although these courses may carry different names and course titles across settings, broadly speaking, they emphasize sociocultural and sociopolitical frameworks and conceptually tie back to the National Latino/a Education Research and Policy Project's (NLERAP's) "Charting a New Course" (Nieto, Rivera, Quiñones, & Irizarry, 2012) statement of what is needed in the future of teacher preparation for an increasing Latina/o demographic in our public schools.

With respect to a sociocultural focus, issues of culture, language, literacy and biliteracy, bilingualism, and multiculturalism are essential elements of study. With respect to a sociopolitical focus, critical race theory and praxis that include the critical content knowledge necessary to be a socially conscious, transformative advocate, educator, and community activist are necessary. Important to both is a participatory action research (PAR) component, which is addressed in Chapters 4 and 5 of this handbook.

The topics, suggested activities, and bibliographies are guideposts to the critical curriculum content that we have developed over many years as Latino and Latina scholar activists. These topics include:

1. Teaching from a social justice paradigm;
2. Naming and interrogating practices and policies in public schools;
3. Critical race theory;
4. Critical pedagogy;
5. Sociocultural teaching/learning theory;
6. Language, literacy, and culture; and
7. Creative praxes.

Likewise, we have learned from our own experiences and those of teacher candidates and veteran teachers that pedagogy is not enough. We have to continuously name and interrogate our own deficit thinking and internalized oppression in order to transform ourselves in these ways. Thus, an underlying premise is to make sure that we address these deficit myths, untruths, and ideologies from the start.

John F. Kennedy once said: "For the greatest enemy of the truth is very often not the lie—deliberate, contrived and dishonest—but the myth—persistent, persuasive, and unrealistic" (Kennedy, 1962). Accordingly, Flores (1982) maintains the following:

It is the new myths that we must stop before they gain an established and "authentic" popularity in our educational and instructional circles. Indeed, myths are persistent because they often are not questioned; they are persuasive because they offer a simplistic view of a complex reality; and they are unrealistic because they disguise the truth.

Our perceptions of reality guide us in explaining it. If reality is perceived from a linear, cause-and-effect gaze, then explanations of reality become simplistic and common sense. But if perceptions of reality take into account the complexity and interrelationships that phenomena share, then construction of reality will certainly differ and may come closer to representing the reality that is being examined.

Most myths are born from linear perceptions of reality (a positivist's view). Myths die from investigating [and interrogating] their origins and relevance to reality when reality is presented from another perspective and by disclosing the invalidity of the myths themselves. (Flores, 1982, pp. 331–332)

The rejection of unfounded and destructive myths will have profound impacts on the teaching/learning and schooling success of children, especially if they are poor, immigrant, and culturally and linguistically diverse. By naming, interrogating, and transforming these myths related to language, culture, class, race, gender, and sexual orientation, teachers will be more likely to organize teaching and learning to their maximum potential instead of creating negative zones of failure.

Our Latina and Latino teachers need to know that the genesis of the deficit point of view as an explanation for Latinos' "lack of success in school and educational achievement" has long historical, cultural, and educational roots (Carter, 1970; Carter & Segura, 1979; Flores, 2005). Anticipating current discourses on "grit" and "growth mindsets" (Kohn, 2015), Romano-V (1967) explains, "No matter from which group they come, those in power describe their own station in life as resulting directly from goal-oriented behavior, a competitive urge . . . in short, they place the reasons or causes of their 'successes' somewhere within themselves" (p. 8). Others, who do not share this orientation or who are not successful, are labeled as inferior. "The reasons or causes of 'inferior' status [are placed] somewhere within the minds, within the personalities, or within the culture of those who are economically, politically or educationally out of power" (p. 7).

The following are some examples of deficit myths that need to be named, interrogated, and transformed:

1. Latino/a and African American students don't do well in school because they are poor.

2. Latino/a and African American students' parents don't care, don't help them at home and can't read, so this is why "these" kids fail in school.
3. Spanish-speaking children need to abandon their first language, identity, and culture in order to "make it" in this society.
4. Learning English guarantees success in society and school.
5. A score on a standardized test actually measures a child's ability in an academic subject.
6. When a child code switches, this means that they do not know either language well.
7. Scripted lessons actually help a teacher to teach students.
8. When a student can read so many words in a minute, this indicates a proficient reader.
9. Racism does not exist among and between Latino families, among and between African American families, and among and between races.
10. Teachers' beliefs, ideologies, and attitudes do not matter when teaching linguistically, culturally, and economically diverse students.

Stereotypes beget prejudice and negativity. Transforming ways of thinking, or, rather, engaging in the metamorphosis of new forms of thinking, will shift our teacher candidates' deficit ideologies so that this new critical curricular knowledge, pedagogy, and community action lead to organizing success in school, at home, and in the community for our all our children and students, especially our Latino children and students.

In the aftermath of decades of scripted curricula, of curricula narrowed to only reading and math, and of teaching focused on isolated skills, our social justice ideology, our critical pedagogical knowledge, and our political will and courage to teach to students' potential are highly needed. Brain-based research (e.g., Caine & Nummela-Caine, 1997; Caine, Nummela-Caine, & Crowell, 1999; Pink, 2006; Sousa, 2011) calls for teaching subjects embedded in rich and meaningful contexts, engaging students and teachers in complex thinking, and foregrounding interesting topics.

Fortunately, brain-based research has caught up with what sociocultural scholars have already known for some time—namely, that a purposeful, rich educational experience that connects to students' lives is essential to a quality educational experience. To this, we add the importance of sociocultural and sociopolitical perspectives in teaching and learning that are grounded in a social justice orientation and are attuned to our students' and their communities' experiences as political, economic, cultural, and social minorities in a country that is sorely in need of the paradigm shift that we present herein (Nieto et al., 2012). Although not exhaustive, the various topics, themes, frameworks, and instructional activities that follow are nevertheless substantial and rooted in the curricular frameworks and experiences that we, as university-level faculty and scholars, regularly provide in the context of the teacher preparation courses that we teach.

TOPIC 1: TEACHING FROM A SOCIAL JUSTICE PARADIGM

A teacher who approaches teaching from a social justice paradigm has made a commitment to instruct in a revolutionary and counter-hegemonic fashion. Such a teacher places students—their lives, voices, perspectives, historical and cultural backgrounds, and emerging cultural formations—at the center of their teaching and learning efforts (hooks, 1994). At the heart of the social justice paradigm is the notion of the teacher as "change agent."

An agent of change views the traditional/typical schooling process as historically inequitable and grounded in a deficit view of students who are culturally and linguistically different. From a traditional perspective, the teacher is the (sole) disseminator of information (i.e., knowledge) and the students are the users of this knowledge. In contrast, a social justice educator views knowledge as mutually constructed and shared (Freire, 1970). This kind of teacher perceives students and their respective communities as places where "knowledge" of a different sort resides, knowledge that is as rich, valid, and relevant as what has traditionally been imparted in K–12 classrooms in the United States. A social justice teacher guides students to become not only productive and contributing citizens but also individuals who will be civically engaged, intellectually critical, and socially conscious.

Themes

- **Critical Consciousness/Political Identity**: This is the initial step in praxis, developing the power and ability to work against oppressive practices. Critical consciousness fosters the ability to think critically about one's own educational experiences. This allows individuals to recognize that their experiences of social and economic inequities are not the result of their individual actions, but rather are derived from larger sociopolitical conditions.

- **Change Agency**: This is a perspective characteristic of individuals who view their professional work in schools and other spaces as driven by critical action aimed at bringing about a more equitable distribution of power, in which access to knowledge is mediated by respectful and affirming pedagogical approaches.
- **Intellectual Empowerment**: This is a process whereby an individual is transformed by an intellectual "enlightenment" and uses his or her new understandings and abilities to promote societal good.
- **Transformational Action**: This refers to a commitment to conscious action and social change using critical frames of analysis (e.g., critical race theory, feminist theory, queer studies, etc.), leading to positive and effective social change.

Guiding Questions

How do teachers come to know about the communities they will be working in? How do teachers name, interrogate, and transform the cultural and linguistic deficit views that are pervasive in the pre-K–12 educational system? How can a social justice paradigm transform traditional educational outcomes from focusing exclusively on developing individual human capital to emphasizing community empowerment for a more equitable and just society?

Sample Activities

Suggested activities include Mini-Ethnography: Community, District, School, and Classroom Study (see Appendix B); Transforming Deficit Myths About Language, Literacy, and Culture (see Appendix C); and Naming, Interrogating, and Transforming Deficit Myths, Fallacies, and "Habitudes" (see Appendix D).

Transformational action example. The Social Justice Education Project students in Tucson, Arizona, created a video revealing the substandard conditions at their school. The students distributed copies of the video to school board members, administrators, teachers, and students. Two months after the release of the video, the principal began to invest money into the school to improve conditions, including repairing bathrooms, ceilings, and water fountains, and updating library materials and technology (see Chapter 4).

Cornerstone Readings

Flores, B. (1982). *Language interference or influence: Toward a theory for Hispanic bilingualism* (Unpublished doctoral dissertation). University of Arizona, Tucson, AZ.

Flores, B. (2005). The intellectual presence of the deficit view of Spanish-speaking children in the educational literature during the 20th century. In P. Pedraza & M. M. Rivera (Eds.), *Latino education: An agenda for community action research* (pp. 75–99). Mahwah, NJ: Erlbaum.

Flores, B., Cousin, P., & Diaz, E. (1991). Transforming deficit myths about learning, language, and culture. *Language Arts, 68*(5), 369–379.

Freire, P. (1970). *Pedagogy of the oppressed.* New York, NY: Bloomsbury Publishing.

Freire, P. (1998). *Teachers as cultural workers: Letters to those who dare teach.* Boulder, CO: Westview Press.

Romano-V, O. I. (1967). Minorities, history and the cultural mystique. *El Grito, 1*(1), 5–11.

Valencia, R. (2010). *Chicano students and the courts: The Mexican American legal struggle for educational equality.* New York, NY: New York University Press.

Valencia, R. (2010). *Dismantling contemporary deficit thinking: Educational thought and practice.* New York, NY: Routledge.

Valenzuela, A. (1999). *Subtractive Schooling: U.S. Mexican youth and the politics of caring.* Albany, NY: State University of New York Press.

Recommended Readings

Ambruster-Sandoval, R. (2005). Is another world possible? Is another classroom possible?: Radical pedagogy, activism, and social change. *Social Justice, 32*(2), 34–51.

Katsarou, E., Picower, B., & Stovall, D. (2010). Acts of solidarity: Developing urban social justice educators in the struggle for quality public education. *Teacher Education Quarterly, 37*(3), 137–153.

Nieto, S., Rivera, M., Quiñones S., & Irizarry, J. (Eds.). (2012). Charting a new course: Understanding the sociocultural, political, economic, and historical context of Latino/a Education in the United States [Special issue]. *Association of Mexican-American Educators (AMAE) Journal, 6*(1).

Wong, P. L., Murai, H., Berta-Ávila, M., William-White, L., Baker, S., Arellano, A., & Echandía, A. (2007). The M/M Center: Meeting the demand for multicultural, multilingual teacher preparation. *Teacher Education Quarterly*, 34(4), 9–25.

TOPIC 2: NAMING AND INTERROGATING PRACTICES AND POLICIES IN PUBLIC SCHOOLS

The American schooling system is steeped in a tradition of imperialism and colonization that is evident in the many educational practices and policies that marginalize historically underrepresented groups, such as Native Americans, African Americans, Puerto Ricans, Mexican Americans, and other Latino groups in the United States. Their ongoing social, economic, political, and cultural marginalization is mirrored in an educational system that overwhelmingly continues to fail them by fostering pedagogical practices and policies that impede innovation, experimentation, and exploration, including those related to the pursuit of alternative pathways needed for addressing the pressing social, economic, cultural, and educational needs of these communities.

Themes

- **Imperialism/Colonization in American Education**: Imperialism/colonization is the fundamental underlying sociopolitical philosophy of the U.S. territorial expansion accomplished through war and Manifest Destiny and is the historical legacy of White supremacy.
- **Marginalized Groups and Schooling Practices**: Public schools were created to reproduce social and economic inequalities; structures such as high-stakes testing, tracking, vocational pathways, and college-readiness programs premised on a rank-ordering and sorting of youth based on socially constructed success (and failure) accomplish this goal.
- **Federal and State Policy** (language, testing, standards, funding): Sociohistorical knowledge developed by naming and interrogating past and present federal and state policies on language, high-stakes testing, standards, tracking, and (inequitable) funding for public schooling provides a

foundation for understanding the negative impact of macro-level educational policy on the Latino community.

Guiding Questions

What were the original purposes and consequences of public schooling? How does schooling impact the social structure? What roles can teachers play in transforming and making history? How do educational policies impact students' lives and teachers' work?

Sample Activities

Conduct a data analysis of the Latino achievement gap, past and present; analyze a federal or state policy that makes it possible to trace the detrimental effects on Latino students' academic outcomes; follow a policy agenda pursued by a teachers' union or association that makes it possible for students to see how external forces influence their teaching and how, as teachers, they are also positioned to be social change agents; research, write, and present biographies of teachers who are agents of change in local community efforts; and examine the role of metaphor in how we understand education and its relationship to colonialism.

Cornerstone Readings

Bettie, J. (2003). *Women without class: Girls, race, and identity*. Oakland, CA: University of California Press.

Bowles, S., & Gintis, H. (1976). *Schooling in capitalist America*. New York, NY: Basic Books, Inc.

Flores-González, N. (2002). *School kids/street kids: Identity development in Latino students*. New York, NY: Teachers College Press.

Pallares, A., & Flores-Gonzalez, N. (2010). *¡Marcha!: Latino Chicago and the immigrant rights movement*. Chicago, IL: University of Illinois Press.

Portes, P. (2005). *Dismantling educational inequality*. Broadway, NY: Peter Lang Publishing.

San Miguel, G. (2000). *Let all of them take heed: Mexican Americans and the campaign for educational equality in Texas, 1910–1981*. College Station, TX: Texas A&M University Press.

San Miguel, G. (2004). *Contested policy: The rise and fall of federal bilingual education in the United States, 1960–2001*. Denton, TX: University of North Texas Press.

Spring, J. (2001). *The American school: 1642–2000* (5th ed.). Boston, MA: McGraw-Hill.

Recommended Readings

Anyon, J. (1980). Social class and the hidden curriculum of work. *Journal of Education, 162*(1), 7–92.

Cammarota, J. (2004). The gendered and racialized pathways of Latina and Latino youth: Different struggles, different resistances. *Anthropology and Education Quarterly, 35*(1), 53–74.

Cammarota, J., & Romero, A. (2014). *Raza studies: The public option for educational revolution.* Tucson, AZ: Arizona University Press.

Foley, D. (2010). *Learning capitalist culture: Deep in the heart of Tejas* (2nd ed.). Philadelphia, PA: University of Pennsylvania Press.

Giroux, H. A. (2003). Education incorporated? In A. Darder, M. P. Baltodano, & R. D. Torres (Eds.), *The critical pedagogy reader* (pp. 119–125). New York, NY: Routledge.

Irizarry, J. (2011). *The Latinization of U.S. schools: Successful teaching and learning in shifting cultural contexts.* Boulder, CO: Paradigm Publishers.

Macedo, D. (2006). *Literacies of power: What Americans are not allowed to know.* Boulder, CO: Westview Press.

Santa Ana, O. (2002). *Brown tide rising: Metaphors of Latinos in contemporary American public discourse.* Austin, TX: University of Texas Press.

Tuck, E., & Yang, K. W. (2012). Decolonization is not a metaphor. *Decolonization: Indigeneity, Education & Society, 1*(1), 1–40.

TOPIC 3: CRITICAL RACE THEORY

Critical race theory is committed to engaging in practical and policy changes that are driven by *analysis of systems of domination,* including race and racism, sexism, classism, and heterosexism, together with their intersectionalities. This perspective challenges dominant ideologies and aims to provide counternarratives to historical and contemporary struggles facing Latinos and other marginalized groups in the United States. A critical theory approach privileges the voices, experiences, and knowledge bases of our communities. And, it focuses our efforts on social justice in our classrooms, schools, and communities.

Themes

- **Racism**: Internalized and institutionalized racism occur on multiple levels; an individual may experience internal psychological effects as well as domination imposed by institutional structures in the form of microagressions. Racism can occur within a single group as well as between two or more groups. For instance, racism exists when family members treat each other differently based on characteristics such as hair texture, pigmentation, eye color, and so forth.

- **Intersectionality**: Race is not experienced in isolation but through its intersection with other social categories (e.g., gender, class, sexuality, undocumented status).
- **Power and Status**: Racism is embedded in social structures that provide individuals who have power and status with privileges and advantages in society.
- **Critical Inquiry**: This approach calls for praxis grounded in decolonizing theories that examine the sociohistorical, sociopolitical, and material contexts and conditions of individuals' lives.
- **Counternarratives**: These are stories that emerge from the lived experiences of marginalized groups. These narratives challenge the hegemonic narratives and discourses that maintain people in positions of domination or subordination.

Guiding Questions

What individuals, literature/readings, and other forms of media can we identify that offer a critical perspective on the historical centrality of race/ethnicity in U.S. society? How and with what consequences does race/ethnicity get manifest through its intersection with other social categories, such as gender, class, sexuality, and undocumented status?

Sample Activities

Complete the BaFa BaFa: Cross-Cultural Diversity/Inclusion Simulation Overview (see Appendix E; the online simulation available at https://www.youtube.com/watch?t=6&v=zW20RcgFxQc is also helpful); read "White Privilege: Unpacking the Invisible Knapsack," by Peggy McIntosh (1990; see Appendix F); conduct an educational dialogue (see Chapter 4, "*PAR Entremundos*: A Practitioner's Guide"); see Anzaldúa (1987), Bartolomé (2006), and Valenzuela (2008) to examine identity, intersectionalities, and internalized oppression and their implications for learning, motivation, and feelings of connectedness to school. Draw on Lipkin (1999) to discuss the implications of sexual orientation for youth of color in schools today. Explore how harassment, bullying, and relationship violence for youth of color intersect with gender, class, sexuality, and undocumented status. Discuss what the UndocuQueer movement teaches us about the cultural worlds that many undocumented students inhabit and that make "coming out" particularly challenging (view and discuss the United We Dream video "UndocuQueer Manifesto," available on YouTube at https://www.youtube.com/ANlKTdTWp4s).

Cornerstone Readings

Anzaldúa, G. (1987). *Borderlands la frontera: The new Mestiza.* San Francisco, CA: Spinsters/Aunt Lute Book Company.

Bartolomé, L. I. (2006). The struggle for language rights: Naming and interrogating the colonial legacy of "English only." *Human Architecture: Journal of the Sociology of Self-Knowledge, 4*(3), 25–32.

Delgado, R., & Stefancic, J. (2001). *Critical race theory: An introduction.* New York, NY: New York University Press.

Fanon, F. (1963). *The wretched of the earth.* New York, NY: The Grove Press.

Freire, P. (1970). *Pedagogy of the oppressed.* New York, NY: Seabury Press.

Hurtado, A. (1989). Relating to privilege: Seduction and rejection in the subordination of White women and women of color. *Signs: Journal of Women in Culture and Society, 14*(4), 833–855.

Lipkin, A. (1999). *Understanding homosexuality, changing schools.* Boulder, CO: Westview Press.

Romero, M. (2012). *The maid's daughter: Living inside and outside the American dream.* New York, NY: New York University Press.

Scheurich, J. J., & Young, M. D. (1997). Coloring epistemologies: Are our research epistemologies racially biased? *Educational Researcher, 26*(4), 4–16.

Seif, H. (2014). "Coming out of the shadows" and "UndocuQueer": Undocumented immigrants transforming sexuality discourse and activism. *Journal of Language and Sexuality, 3*(1), 87–120.

Solorzano, D. G., & Bernal, D. D. (2001). Examining transformational resistance through a critical race and LatCrit theory framework Chicana and Chicano students in an urban context. *Urban Education, 36*(3), 308–342.

Valenzuela, A. (2008). Uncovering internalized oppression. In M. P. Pollock (Ed.), *Everyday antiracism: Concrete strategies for successfully navigating the relevance of race in school* (pp. 50–55). New York, NY: The New Press.

Recommended Readings

Berta-Avila, M., Tijerina-Revilla, A., & Figueroa, J. (Eds.). (2011). *Marching students: Chicana and Chicano activism in education, 1968 to the present.* Reno, NV: University of Nevada Press.

Brayboy, B. M. J. (2006). Toward a tribal critical race theory in education. *Urban Review, 37*(5), 425–446.

Delgado-Bernal, D. (2002). Critical race theory, Latino critical theory, and critical raced-gendered epistemologies: Recognizing students of color as holders and creators of knowledge. *Qualitative Inquiry, 8,* 105–246.

Foster, M. (1990). The politics of race: Through the eyes of African-American teachers. *Journal of Education, 172*(3), 123–141.

Holland, S. P. (2005). The last word on racism: New directions for a critical race theory. *South Atlantic Quarterly, 104*(3), 403–423.

Jewett, S. (2006). "If you don't identify with your ancestry, you're like a race without a land": Constructing race at a small urban middle school. *Anthropology & Education Quarterly, 37,* 144–161.

Ladson-Billings, G., & Tate, W. F. (1995). Toward a critical race theory of education. *Teachers College Record, 97,* 47–68.

Matias, C. E. (2013). Tears worth telling: Urban teaching and the possibilities of racial justice, *Multicultural Perspectives, 15*(4), 187–193.

Rodríguez, L. F. (2012). "Everybody grieves, but still nobody sees": Toward a theory of recognition for students of color in U.S. education. *Teachers College Record, 114*(1), 1–31.

Tate, W. F. (1997). Critical race theory and education: History, theory, and implications. *Review of Research in Education, 22,* 195–247.

Yosso, T. J., Parker, L., Solorzano, D. G., & Lynn, M. (2004). From Jim Crow to affirmative action and back again: A critical race discussion of racialized rationales and access to higher education. *Review of Research in Education, 28*(1), 1–25.

TOPIC 4: CRITICAL PEDAGOGY

Critical pedagogy includes creating democratic, equitable relationships in which teachers and students work collectively to co-construct knowledge and action. Teachers who use critical pedagogy employ dialogical and praxis-oriented methods, foster students' identity development, and tap the wealth of resources available in communities and from other adults who know their students. In addition, these teachers use critical reflection and act as "pedagogic militants" (Gouvea,

1998) who achieve social justice outcomes by providing a high-quality and culturally relevant education to those least valued by our school systems and society.

Themes

- **Engaged Participants**: Practitioners and community members should be involved in all aspects of teaching, learning, and inquiry, and they should be involved as full participants.
- **Knowledge Co-construction**: Knowledge that informs action should be produced in collaboration with communities where engaged practitioners, students, and community members become a collective of knowledge producers/actors.
- **Critical Reflection**: Engaged practitioners should critically reflect on their own processes, foster trusting relationships of mutuality, examine power within the community, and engage in deep self-inquiry.
- **Ideological Clarity**: This involves rejecting assimilationist and deficit views of immigrant and minority students and questioning romanticized views of the dominant culture. It entails explorations into the cultural wealth that exists in students' communities while interrogating meritocratic explanations of the dominant social order and becoming cultural border crossers.
- **Transformational Action**: This involves a commitment to conscious action and social change, using creative praxes and engaged policy.

Guiding Questions

How does knowledge co-construction first take place and then continue to cycle throughout the teaching and learning process? How can teachers share power and provide the tools for students' self-empowerment? What can teachers do to provide and maintain a high-quality, culturally relevant pedagogy?

Sample Activities

Explore, discuss, and list aspects of the community cultural wealth of the local community. Consider ways that students' parents possess community cultural wealth and how this can be useful to the classroom. Conduct a dialogical pedagogy or problem tree exercise (see Chapter 4, *"PAR Entremundos*: A Practitioner's Guide"). Conduct the Critical Pedagogy Framework for Creative Reflection exercise (see Appendix G; also see Root Causes example in Chapter 4).

Cornerstone Readings

Bartolomé, L. (2007). *Ideologies in education: Unmasking the trap of teacher neutrality.* Broadway, NY: Peter Lang Publishing.

Cammarota, J., & Fine, M. (Eds.). (2008). *Revolutionizing education: Youth participatory action research in motion.* New York, NY: Routledge.

Freire, P. (1970). *Pedagogy of the oppressed.* New York, NY: Seabury Press.

Freire, P. (1998). *Pedagogy of freedom: Ethics, democracy, and civic courage.* New York, NY: Rowman & Littlefield.

Freire, P., & Macedo, D. (1987). *Literacy: Reading the world and the word.* Westport, CT: Praeger.

Mitchie, G. (2009). *Holler if you hear me: The education of a teacher and his students* (2nd ed.). New York, NY: Teacher College Press.

Yosso, T. J. (2005). Whose culture has capital? A critical race theory discussion of community cultural wealth. *Race, Ethnicity, and Education, 8*(1), 69–91.

Recommended Readings

Foley, D. E., & Valenzuela, A. (2005). Critical ethnography: The politics of collaboration. In N. K. Denzin & Y. Lincoln (Eds.), *The handbook of qualitative research* (3rd ed., pp. 217–234). Beverly Hills, CA: Sage Publications.

Green, M. (2003). In search of a critical pedagogy. In A. Darder, M. Baltodano, & R. D. Torres (Eds.), *The critical pedagogy reader* (pp. 97–112). New York, NY: Routledge Falmer.

Larrotta, C., & Yamamura, E. K. (2011). A community cultural wealth approach to Latina/Latino parent involvement: The promise of family literacy. *Adult Basic Education and Literacy Journal, 5*(2), 74–83.

Liou, D. D., Antrop-González, R., & Cooper, R. (2009). Unveiling the promise of community cultural wealth to sustaining Latina/o students' college-going information networks. *Educational Studies, 45*(6), 534–555.

López, P. D., Valenzuela, A., & Garcia, E. (2011). The critical ethnography for public policy. In B. U. Levinson & M. Pollock (Eds.), *Companion to the anthropology of education* (pp. 547–563). Maiden, MA: Wiley-Blackwell Press.

McLaren, P. (2003). Critical pedagogy: A look at the major concepts. In A. Darder, M., Baltodano, & R. D. Torres (Eds.), *The critical pedagogy reader* (pp. 119–125). New York, NY: Routledge Falmer.

Rivera, K. M. (1999). Popular research and social transformation: A community-based approach to critical pedagogy. *TESOL Quarterly, 33*(3), 485–500.

Valenzuela, A. (Ed.). (2005). *Leaving children behind: How "Texas-style" accountability fails Latino youth.* Albany, NY: State University of New York Press.

Yosso, T., & García, D. (2007). "This is no slum!": A critical race theory analysis of community cultural wealth in Culture Clash's Chavez Ravine. *Aztlan: A Journal of Chicano Studies, 32*(1), 145–179.

Zambrana, R. E., & Zoppi, I. M. (2002). Latina students: Translating cultural wealth into social capital to improve academic success. *Journal of Ethnic and Cultural Diversity in Social Work, 11*(1–2), 33–53.

TOPIC 5: SOCIOCULTURAL TEACHING AND LEARNING THEORY

L. S. Vygotsky's sociocultural theoretical framework for understanding the interrelationship among teaching, learning, and development provides the basis for organizing teaching and learning to maximum potential (Vygotsky, 1978). There are several concepts associated with Vygotsky's approach that educators need to understand: sociocultural construction of knowledge, the zone of proximal development, mediation, appropriation, internalization, and creativity. Putting these concepts to use will bring about a shift in teachers' pedagogical knowledge and ways of teaching. Just as importantly, it also will result in learning successes for students, as evidenced by their uses of new knowledge across many contexts, including in reading and writing expository and narrative texts; in subject areas such as science, mathematics, and social studies; and in the visual and performing arts (Mendoza-Reis & Flores, 2014). Vygotsky has been particularly influential on the thinking, theorizing, and writings of NLERAP scholars (e.g., Moll, 1992; González, Moll, & Amanti, 2005), and thus on our philosophical approach to learning as a whole.

Themes

- **Sociocultural Knowledge Construction**: Vygotsky (1978) posited that knowledge is socially constructed through social interaction. Knowledge is first shared between people and then internalized within an individual's own psychological realm. This sociocultural framework is pivotal and basic because it challenges the individualistic psychological assumptions that underlie many of the learning theories that dominate American education.

- **Culturally Responsive Pedagogy**: Culturally responsive education recognizes, respects, and uses students' identities and backgrounds as meaningful sources for creating optimal learning environments.
- **Funds of Knowledge**: By becoming familiar with their students' communities and families, teachers will discover the cultural, social, and cognitive resources (funds of knowledge) Latino students bring with them. Teachers should organize their teaching/learning to build upon these assets.
- **Vygotsky's Zone of Proximal Development, Mediation, Appropriation, Internalization, and Creativity**: These sociocultural concepts are vital in organizing teaching and learning to address students' potential level of development instead of their current, demonstrated developmental level. The zone of proximal development simply delineates the distance between these two stages in students' acquisition of knowledge. Mediation involves a teacher's or a more capable peer's use of psychological tools to help create a bridge from the known (i.e., the knowledge that the child already possesses) to new knowledge. Appropriation occurs as individuals make new knowledge their own. Internalization refers to the process through which an activity that was external becomes internal. Students can then create and innovate beyond the knowledge that was internalized.

Guiding Questions

What are the disconnections between how we learn and how we are taught in schools? How is knowledge constructed, and whose knowledge is valued? What is the role of social interaction in teaching and learning? How can the teacher serve as a deliberate mediator rather than a technician, authoritarian, or banker of knowledge?

Sample Activities

Conduct the Group Work and Second Language Learner Planner activity (see Appendix H), using the Productive Group Work Rubric (see Appendix I). The second language learner planner is an organizing tool that has teachers consider the language demands of a topic or concept to be taught, for example, in the area of writing, reading, listening, or speaking. The planner asks teachers to identify the specific skills and support scaffolds to be taught in order to support the language demands asked of their students, thus enabling them to access the content while continuing their development of the academic language. Once teachers complete this work via the planner, it can in turn be incorporated into their lessons plans.

Cornerstone Readings

Gay, G. (2010). *Culturally responsive teaching: Theory, research, and practice.* New York, NY: Teachers College Press.

González, N., Moll, L. C., & Amanti, C. (2005). *Funds of knowledge: Theorizing practices in households, communities and classrooms.* Mahwah, NJ: Lawrence Erlbaum Associates.

Nieto, S. (2007). *Affirming diversity: The sociopolitical context of multicultural education* (5th ed.). Boston, MA: Allyn & Bacon.

Villegas, A. M., & Lucas, T. (2007). The culturally responsive teacher. *Educational Leadership, 64*(6), 28–33.

Vygotsky, L. S. (1978). *Mind and society: The development of higher mental processes.* Cambridge, MA: Harvard University Press.

Recommended Readings

Cohen, E. G. (1994). *Designing groupwork: Strategies for the heterogeneous classroom.* New York, NY: Teachers College Press.

Frey, N., Fisher, D., & Everlove, S. (2009). *Productive group work: How to engage students, build teamwork, and promote understanding.* Alexandria, VA: ASCD.

Ladson-Billings, G. (2009). *The dreamkeepers: Successful teachers of African American children* (2nd ed.). San Francisco, CA: John Wiley & Sons.

Mendoza Reis, N., & Flores, B. (2014). Changing the pedagogical culture of schools with Latino English language learners: Reculturing instructional leadership. In P. R. Portes, S. Salas, P. Baquedano-López, & P. J. Mellom (Eds.), *U.S. Latinos in K–12 education: Seminal research-based policy directions for change we can believe in.* Charlotte, NC: Information Age Publishing.

Moll, L. C. (1992). *Vygotsky and education: Instructional implications and applications of sociohistorical psychology.* Cambridge, England: Cambridge University Press.

Portes, P., & Salas, S. (2011). *Vygotsky in 21st century society.* Broadway, NY: Peter Lang.

TOPIC 6: LANGUAGE, LITERACY, AND CULTURE

It would be impossible to adequately address any of the previous themes absent a clear understanding of and appreciation for the inter-related nature of language, literacy, and culture. Teaching and learning processes are primarily mediated through language and literacy, which are in turn culturally imbued. Knowledge of how culture shapes and is shaped by literacy practices in the pre-K–12 classroom and in students' home communities is key for teachers who advocate student and community participation, support students' social identity and expression, and design instruction that addresses the ideologies and power relations needed to transform schools, communities, and the broader society (Herrera, Pérez, & Escamilla, 2011). Moreover, Latina and Latino teachers who will most likely work with CLD students who also may be English language learners must be well prepared to teach language and literacy from a perspective that considers the multiple dimensions—including sociocultural, linguistic, and academic backgrounds—that influence their students' language and literacy development.

Themes

- **Language-Acquisition Theories: Language 1 (L1)/
  Language 2 (L2)**: Effective teachers of CLD students
  understand the processes and stages involved in second
  language acquisition and their relationship to how children
  acquire their first language. This knowledge provides
  insights regarding which literacy skills transfer to the second
  language, and it builds teachers' capacity to pinpoint a
  student's specific gaps in language development and academic
  skills (Echevarría, Vogt, & Short, 2004; Merino, Trueba, &
  Samaniego, 1993; Wong Fillmore & Snow, 2002). This is
  particularly critical for secondary-level teachers working
  with CLD adolescents. These students typically present a
  wide range of L1 and L2 literacy habits and skills, possess
  varying depths of content-area knowledge, and come from
  vastly different family and schooling backgrounds (Meltzer &
  Hamann, 2005).
- **Bilingualism/Biliteracy**: Advocacy for CLD students whose
  first language is not English includes promoting bilingualism

and biliteracy through support and implementation of highly rigorous pedagogy that values and leverages the students' native languages. Effective teachers of Latinos and other CLD students understand that language and literacy practices develop within sociocultural contexts through which meaning is constructed. Therefore, they encourage students' use of their first language not solely for language-acquisition purposes but also as the basis for students' critical comprehension and expression.

- **The Proficient Reading Process**: Kenneth Goodman (Goodman, 1976, 1982, 1996; Goodman & Goodman, 2013) and many other scholars around the world have conducted research on proficient reading over the last 45 years. Today, we know what proficient reading looks and sounds like at all levels of schooling. If secondary students are not proficient readers, they will face insurmountable challenges across the curriculum. Therefore, it is imperative that content teachers understand and know how to organize, scaffold/mediate, and assess students' teaching and learning experiences. This is essential in order to not only develop the secondary L1 and L2 learners as proficient readers across different texts and genres, but also to teach so that the students acquire academic language in the expository domains.

- **Pedagogical Scaffolding**: The adolescent language learner faces the double challenge of learning a second language while also learning core subject-matter concepts, for the most part, in that second language (Short & Fitzsimmons, 2007). For teachers, the implications of this daunting combination are many, not the least of which is how to design instruction that is intellectually rigorous and challenging and yet simultaneously supportive of CLD students' language and literacy development (Gibbons, 2009). Scaffolding includes strategic planning, with integrated content and language objectives. Objectives are based on the students' particular strengths, interests, and needs, along with a deep understanding of the language and literacy demands of their curriculum subject, materials, and so forth. The teacher then uses this knowledge to include scaffolds to temporarily support students' learning through each phase of the learning process

(Echevarría, Vogt, & Short, 2010). Assessment in such a context is not an event, but rather an everyday affair. It is a planned and intentional component of classroom instruction (National Council of Teachers of English, 2013). For a deeper examination of assessment, see Lavadenz (1996), who makes a cogent argument for authentic assessment and providing immediate feedback to students, ideally in the actual learning context.

- **Academic Language**: Academic language refers to the ways of knowing, thinking, and communicating that are specific to the schooling context. This includes but goes beyond the learning of discipline-specific vocabulary. Academic language also refers to grammatical structures and conventions, types of written and oral texts, and discourse skills. Extending students' voices is a key aspect. Academic language and literacy practices have been linked to academic success. Too often, CLD students' diverse ways of knowing, thinking, and speaking diverge significantly from those that are prioritized in school (Gee, 1996). Teachers of CLD students both value and build upon the cultural and linguistic capital that the students bring to school from home and community, while at the same time adding academic and discipline-specific proficiencies to students' ever-extending repertoires of language and literacy skills (Zwiers, 2008).

Guiding Questions

Why is understanding students' language proficiency and cultural background so important for designing effective instruction? What are the most effective ways to build upon the students' first language and culture? What kinds of pedagogical scaffolds are necessary to provide explicit support and create a productive learning environment for English language learners? How can teachers authentically integrate the teaching of academic language and content to make them mutually supportive? What does a proficient secondary L1 and L2 reader look and sound like across different texts and genres? What is the sociopsycholinguistic theory of reading, and why is it important to understand and know? How can secondary-level content teachers scaffold/mediate the acquisition of proficient reading and academic language in their content areas?

Sample Activities

Complete the Planning for Language and Content Integration tool (see Appendix J). This lesson planning tool supports preservice candidates in identifying the specific language and literacy demands (both function and form) of a discipline-specific lesson. More specifically, it asks candidates to consider the following: (1) Given my content objectives, what are the language demands that must be addressed in order for my students to successfully access, participate in, and demonstrate learning? (2) What language objectives (and corresponding strategies/ activities) will I develop in order to target academic language learning in support of my content teaching?

Cornerstone Readings

Echevarría, J., Vogt, M., & Short, D. J. (2010). *Making content comprehensible for secondary English learners: The SIOP model.* Boston, MA: Pearson Education.

Flurkey, A. D., & Xu, J. (2003). *On the revolution of reading: The selected writings of Kenneth S. Goodman.* Portsmouth, NH: Heinemann.

Gibbons, P. (2009). *English learners, academic literacy and thinking: Learning in the challenge zone.* Portsmouth, NH: Heinemann.

González, N. (2006). *I am my language: Discourses of women and children in the borderlands.* Tucson, AZ: University of Arizona Press.

Goodman, Y., & Marek, A. (1996). *Retrospective miscue analysis: Revaluing readers and reading.* Somers, NY: Richard C. Owen.

Herrera, S. C., Perez, D. R., & Escamilla, K. (2011). *Teaching reading to English language learners.* Boston, MA: Allyn & Bacon.

Lavadenz, M. (2010). From theory to practice for teachers of English learners. *The CATESOL Journal, 22*(1), 18–47.

Lightbrown, P. M., & Spada, N. (1999). *How languages are learned.* London, England: Oxford University Press.

Meltzer, J., & Hamann, E. T. (2005). *Meeting the development needs of English language learners through literacy instruction. Part 2: Focus on classroom teaching and learning strategies* (Paper 53, faculty publications). Lincoln, NB: University of Nebraska–Lincoln, Department of Teaching, Learning and Teacher Education. Retrieved from http://digitalcommons.unl.edu/ teachlearnfacpub/53

Short, D. J., & Fitzsimmons, S. (2007). *Double the work: Challenges and solutions to acquiring language and academic literacy for adolescent English language learners—a report commissioned by the Carnegie Corporation of New York.* Washington, DC: Alliance for Excellent Education.

Walqui, A., & Van Lier, L. (2010). *Scaffolding the academic success of adolescent English language learners: A pedagogy of promise*. San Francisco, CA: WestEd.

Zwiers, J. (2008). *Building academic language: Essential practices for content classrooms*. San Francisco, CA: Jossey-Bass.

Recommended Readings

Delpit, L., & Dowdy, J. K. (Eds.). (2002). *The skin that we speak: Thoughts on language and culture in the classroom*. New York, NY: The New Press.

Gee, J. (1996). *Social linguistics and literacies: Ideology in discourses* (2nd ed.). London, England: Routledge Falmer.

Goodman, K. S. (1976). Reading: A psycholinguistic guessing game. In H. Singer & R. B. Ruddell (Eds.), *Theoretical models and processes of reading* (pp. 497–508). Newark, DE: International Reading Association.

Goodman, K. S. (1982). *Language and literacy: Selected readings of Kenneth S. Goodman*. Boston, MA: Routledge, Kegan & Paul.

Goodman, K. S. (1996). *On reading*. Portsmouth, NH: Heinemann.

Goodman, K. S., & Goodman, Y. (2013). *Making sense of learners making sense of written language: The selected works of Kenneth S. Goodman and Yetta M. Goodman*. New York, NY: Routledge.

Mercer, J., & Hamann, E. T. (2005). *Meeting the literacy development needs of adolescent language learners through content-area learning. Part 2: Focus on developing academic literacy habits and skills across the content*. Providence, RI: Northeast and Islands Regional Educational Laboratory, The Educational Alliance at Brown University. Retrieved from http://www.alliance.brown.edu

Wong Filmore, L., & Snow, C. (2000). *What teachers need to know about language*. Washington, DC: ERIC Clearinghouse on Languages and Linguistics.

TOPIC 7: CREATIVE PRAXES

Methods for teaching/learning within a creative praxis framework are embedded in the cultural and creative productions of the local community. These productions may include poetry, music, dance, theater, and other forms of cultural and artistic expression.

Themes

- **Indigenous Cosmologies**: The use of indigenous cosmologies provides a way to reclaim and reimagine indigenous ways of

knowing and engaging as a healing and community-building
process.

- **Identity/Self-Knowledge**: It is crucial to know how one
  is situated in the world, the meaning of *mestizaje* (i.e., the
  social meanings of blood mixture), how one's culture and
  history inform subjectivity, and how one can contribute to
  society.
- **Reimagining Our Worlds**: This is a process of thinking
  creatively/using a creative lens to reimagine where and how
  we live in order to produce a more humane and equitable
  society.
- **Healing Through the Arts**: This is a process that uses
  the visual and performing arts to heal from the damage
  of oppression.

Guiding Questions

How do the community's cultural arts speak to social and economic
problems that stand in the way of a healthy existence? For example,
is muralism an active form of youth expression? If so, what messages are conveyed within this form of expression? Who are the
audiences for these messages? What is the history of muralism in
the community? How is this form of expression received in the community? In what ways is this form of expression an exercise in individual and community identity? What are the ways of being and
knowing embedded in local creative expression (i.e., localized funds
of knowledge)? How can art inspire personal agency to bring about
change in the world? How does creativity initiate a process of imagination that leads to utopian visions of life? How does artistic expression heal the suffering inflicted by social and economic oppression?
In what ways do identity, spirituality, and social justice find expression in art that emanates from the community? How is indigeneity
as a way of knowing reflected in artistic expression? How is an indigenous identity, as opposed to a national origin or racial identity,
an empowering one?

Sample Activities

Use maps, PhotoVoice, video documentary, poetry, informal conversations, play, community performance theater, and other activities

as described in Chapter 4. Read chapters 1 and 2 in Colín's (2014) *Mexica Education* and compare and contrast Mexica society with a modern "church community" (also see Luna, 2011). How do their respective rituals, values, and activities overlap, and how do they differ? Then discuss contemporary Mexica's culturally based vision for survival and resistance, together with any fresh insights that a quick review of Mexica cultural roots and identity provide. Complement this reading with Valenzuela, Zamora, and Rubio's (2015) examination of *danza Mexica* as part of a larger cultural and linguistic revitalization project in Austin, Texas. Consider what value is added by incorporating indigenous ways of knowing in the context of educational projects that are already attuned to addressing the cultural and linguistic needs, challenges, and opportunities faced by Latino children and youth.

Cornerstone Readings

Batalla, G. B. (1996). *México profundo: Reclaiming a civilization.* Austin, TX: University of Texas Press.

Boal, A. (2008). *Theater of the oppressed.* London, England: Pluto Press.

Cintli Rodriguez, R. (2014). *Our sacred maíz is our mother: Indigeneity and belonging in the Americas.* Tucson, AZ: University of Arizona Press.

Colín, E. (2014). *Indigenous education through dance and ceremony: A Mexica palimpsest.* New York, NY: Palgrave Macmillan.

Elenes, A. C. (2010). *Transforming borders: Chicana/o popular culture and pedagogy.* Lanham, MD: Lexington Books.

Rivera, M., Medellín-Paz, C., & Pedraza, P. (2010). *Imagination for the imagined nation. A creative justice approach to learning.* New York, NY: Center for Puerto Rican Studies, Hunter College, City University of New York.

Rivera, M., & Pedraza, P. (2000). The spirit of transformation: An education reform movement in a New York City Latino community. In S. Nieto (Ed.), *Puerto Rican students in U.S. schools* (pp. 3–10). Mahwah, NJ: Lawrence Erlbaum Associates.

Urrieta, Jr., L. (2003). Las identidades también lloran/Identities also cry: Exploring the human side of Latina/o indigenous identities. *Educational Studies, 34*(2), 148–168.

Valenzuela, A., Zamora, E., & Rubio, B. (2015). Academia Cuauhtli and the eagle: Danza Mexica and the epistemology of the circle. *Voices in Urban Education, 41,* 46–56.

Zander, R., & Zander, B. (2002). *The art of possibility: Transforming professional and personal life.* New York, NY: Penguin Books.

Recommended Readings

Arrien, A. (1993). *The four-fold way: Walking the paths of the warrior, teacher, healer and visionary.* New York, NY: HarperOne.

Cajete, G. (1994). *Look to the mountain: An ecology of Indigenous education.* Asheville, NC: Kivaki Press.

Cajete, G., & Little Bear, L. (1999). *Native science: Natural laws of interdependence.* Santa Fe, NM: Clear Light Publishers.

Csikzentmihalyi, M. (1990). *Flow. The psychology of optimal experience.* New York, NY: Harper Perennial.

Csikzentmihalyi, M. (1996). *Creativity, flow and the psychology of discovery and invention.* New York, NY: Harper Collins.

Denzin, N. K., Lincoln, Y. S., & Smith, L.T. (2008). *Handbook of critical and Indigenous methodologies.* Beverly Hills, CA: Sage.

Greene, M. (1995). *Releasing the imagination: Essays on education, the arts, and social change.* CA: Jossey-Bass.

Jenoure, T. (2000). *Navigators: African American musicians, dancers and visual artists in academe.* Albany, NY: State University of New York Press.

Kelley, R. D. G. (2002). *Freedom dreams: The Black radical imagination.* Boston, MA: Beacon Press.

Pedraza, P., & Rivera, M. (2005). *Latino education: An agenda for community action research: A volume of the National Latino/a Education Research and Policy Project.* Philadelphia, PA: Lawrence Erlbaum Associates.

Smith, L. T. (1999). *Decolonizing methodologies: Research and Indigenous peoples.* London, England: Zed Books.

Torre, M. E., & Ayala J. (2009). Envisioning participatory action research *entremundos. Feminism & Psychology, 19,* 387–393.

Wilson, S. (2008). *Research is ceremony: Indigenous research methods.* Black Point, Nova Scotia: Fernwood Publishing Co.

CHAPTER 4

PAR Entremundos
A Practitioner's Guide

Julio Cammarota, Margarita Berta-Ávila,
Jennifer Ayala, Melissa Rivera, and Louie Rodríguez

This chapter presents information aimed at guiding educators and students in designing and implementing participatory action research (PAR) projects. Because each project has a particular set of needs, here we seek only to inspire ideas and offer a framework for initiating a unique PAR process. In other words, our discussion of PAR should not be read as an exact formula for doing the work. Rather, it is a general reference for action-based inquiries that focus on specific contexts, with particular strengths and challenges. Because of its liberating potential, we of course hope that PAR becomes a regular feature of teacher preparation programs everywhere.

We have divided our discussion of PAR into Chapters 4 and 5 of this volume to help educators and students more quickly grasp the different conditions and parameters for undertaking PAR. The Practitioner's Guide was created by the National Latino/a Education Research and Policy Project (NLERAP) PAR committee. The concept of a *PAR Entremundos* (or PAR among worlds), introduced by Torre and Ayala (2009) and based on Anzaldúa's writings (1987, 1997; Keating, 2009), is further developed and elaborated within a teacher training context in a volume by Ayala et al. (forthcoming). The PAR Practitioner's Guide we refer to here is an extension of the work in *PAR Entremundos*.

The guide provides several principles to channel the work through a critical consciousness lens while establishing democratic, equitable relationships among participants. These principles are explained through theoretical lineages that delineate PAR's ontology and epistemology. With these serving as a foundation, *PAR Entremundos* provides a developmental progression of key questions and activities to prepare those interested in applying a PAR approach to action-based inquiries.

The next chapter (Chapter 5) builds on the Practitioner's Guide with an example of a PAR project, called the Social Justice Education Project (SJEP), conducted in a high school classroom. The SJEP gained notoriety as the capstone course for the Tucson Unified School District's (TUSD) Mexican American Studies (MAS) program after the Arizona state legislature passed a bill (HB 2281) that banned ethnic studies courses that allegedly promoted the overthrow of the U.S. government or promoted resentment toward a particular racial group. The Arizona Department of Education (ADE) declared that the MAS was in violation of ARS 15-112C(A) (anti–ethnic studies law) and threatened to remove 10% of state funds to the district. In January 2012, the TUSD governing board voted in favor of suspending all MAS courses, including the SJEP, to avoid forfeiting 10% of its budget. The ADE forced the district to shut down the SJEP, despite its success for well over a decade in helping students to achieve and become engaged in changing their schools and communities. The SJEP was discontinued in 2011. As of 2015, only one high school in TUSD teaches a single section of the preexisting curriculum.

The SJEP example focuses on students who address and challenge language discrimination at their schools as they move through the developmental progression that is emphasized in this chapter, the Practitioner's Guide. Specifically, the students identify generative themes, collect data, analyze data, and present research results to the community. The ultimate goal of the SJEP is to involve the community in solving the problem of language discrimination in education.

It should also be noted that Appendix K ("PAR Process Handout") of this handbook provides a four-page handout that identifies and summarizes key phases for implementing a PAR project. Using the SJEP case as an example, the phases mark the various research and educational practices involved in completing a PAR process in the classroom. After reading and thinking about both chapters, as well as reviewing the contents of Appendices K ("PAR Process Handout") and L ("Frequently Asked Questions About PAR"), educators and students should have a solid foundation from which to build their own work in this liberating and transformative tradition. This guide draws from *PAR Entremundos* (Ayala et al., forthcoming), a book that introduces a transformative approach to teaching and learning by interweaving education, research, and social action. This Practitioner's Guide provides practitioners with principles and with pedagogical and curricular activities for creating PAR initiatives. The guide is divided into four subsections, as follows:

1. **Overview of PAR:** This explains what PAR entails and describes some of its theoretical lineages.
2. **Guiding Principles:** This subsection identifies eight general principles that guide the collective inquiry in which PAR is grounded.
3. **Guiding Questions and Practices:** This subsection provides questions, examples, and activities tied to the PAR guiding principles. These practices and questions can be used to inform and shape curriculum and pedagogy.
4. **Research Process:** This subsection lists potential methods for data collection, analysis, and dissemination, along with an example of one research process.

OVERVIEW OF PAR

Research in communities has traditionally provided a way for "outsiders" to study the particulars of a community in the name of objective science. In this tradition, a researcher picks a topic, comes into a space, studies it, leaves, and then draws conclusions, with little input from those who were being studied and little interest in making a contribution to the community itself.

PAR turns this view upside down by making the researchers and those being researched partners in the inquiry process. This means that the group as a whole—the researchers and the researched—make decisions collectively. For example, decisions are collectively made about what to study and how to study it, as well as what kind of knowledge will be the goal of the study and what kind of action(s) will be taken in response to the knowledge gained. The research collective is usually made up of people who are interested in a particular equity- or justice-related issue or who are deeply affected in some way by it. The thinking behind this approach is that those who are most affected by inequities or injustices have important insights and knowledge about how to apply remedies. Therefore, this group should play an important part in the research process and outcome(s). In research that focuses on schooling and educational contexts, the "most affected" groups often include students, which is why PAR includes a subfield called YPAR (where Y stands for *youth*).

PAR is not new. We can trace its ancestry across many years and multiple disciplines. NLERAP's approach to PAR, building on what Torre and Ayala (2009) have termed *PAR Entremundos*, is steeped in Freirean praxis, critical race and borderland theories, creative processes and wisdom traditions, South American liberation psychologies, and social movement histories. The four theoretical and conceptual lineages are described in the following subsections.

Southern Tradition

Our PAR work is rooted in what some have termed the southern (hemisphere) tradition of PAR, which incorporates Freire's (1970) notion of praxis. Praxis is the process by which *critical reflection* and *creative, conscious action* are combined to formulate an approach to gaining knowledge that is then utilized for initiating change. Praxis involves critically examining a situation and then taking action to bring about changes that lead to equitable social and economic outcomes. The experience of initiating change produces knowledge that in turn improves critical thinking about the situation and creates possibilities for facilitating change (Fals-Borda & Rahman, 1991).

Critical Race Theory

PAR Entremundos is vigorously committed to engaging in practical and policy changes that are driven by an analysis of systems of domination, including race and racism, sexism, classism, and heterosexism, and their intersectionalities. *PAR Entremundos* challenges dominant ideologies as it aims to provide counternarratives to historical and contemporary struggles facing Latinos/as and other marginalized groups in the United States (Delgado & Stefancic, 1999; Solórzano & Yosso, 2002), privileging the voices, experiences, and knowledge bases of our communities and focusing efforts on social justice in our classrooms, schools, and communities (Berta-Ávila, Tijerina-Revilla, & Figueroa, 2011; Cammarota & Fine, 2008; Irizarry, 2011; Rivera, Medellín-Paz, & Pedraza, 2010).

Feminist Theorizing

Our feminist lineages underscore the ideas related to standpoint, intersectionalities, and embodiment. The positions we hold within our social, cultural, and political contexts situate the knowledge we create, influence the angles we see, and impact the connections we make. Therefore, it is important to acknowledge who we are in relation to the work we do (Collins, 1991; hooks, 1984; Hurtado, 1996). A feminist perspective also encourages us to *theorize from the flesh*, as Moraga and Anzaldúa (1981) viscerally write, to build understandings, theories, and knowledge from the pain, exploitation, resistance, and joy we have lived through our bodies and spirit (Lara, 2002). It reminds us that there are multiple, interacting perspectives that inform our truths—a living dialectic, as it were.

Indigenous Cosmologies

PAR Entremundos also seeks to reclaim and reshape (for the modern era) *wisdom from ancient traditions*. The aim is to awaken spiritual activism by integrating body/mind/spirit (Facio & Lara, 2014; Lara, 2002); using healing arts and the medicine of song, dance, story, and silence (Arrien, 1993); and asking timeless questions, such as, Who am I? What is life? What do I seek from life? (Ponce de Leon Paiva, 1992).

PAR GUIDING PRINCIPLES

In the context of schooling, part of the goal of the *PAR Entremundos* approach is to co-create transformative spaces of education through collectives of research and social action. These collectives include youth, educators, and community members as partners in inquiry and action-based processes focused on addressing educational disparities. We expect this approach to produce more meaningful research and community activism as a whole. In addition, the power of the process itself can have a deep impact on the individuals undertaking it. Those who participate in PAR are often transformed when they recognize their potential to produce knowledge that can foster change. Thus, PAR is ultimately a systematic and collective approach to inquiry (using PAR guiding principles) that leads to the production of knowledge applied for the purpose of facilitating greater equity and justice.

The following are some general principles that, building on the work of NLERAP's PAR committee, guide our view of PAR as *Entremundos*:

Participation. Practitioners and stakeholders should be involved in all steps of research (design, data collection, analysis, dissemination), as full participants in the process (versus as subjects).

Critical inquiry. The work needs to be grounded in critical race and decolonizing theories, which examine the sociohistorical, sociopolitical, and material contexts and conditions of our lives.

Knowledge co-construction. Knowledge that informs action is produced in collaboration with communities, where researchers and researched become a collective of knowledge producers/actors.

Power with(in). The collective critically reflects its own process, fosters trusting relationships of mutuality between members, examines power within the group, and engages in deep self-inquiry.

Indigenous cosmologies. In the spirit of an approach to PAR that is *Entremundos* and that grows from the southern tradition, we see it as a way to reclaim and reimagine indigenous ways of knowing, and engaging in this work as a healing process for the individual and community.

Creative praxes. The methods for collecting and presenting data are embedded in the cultural and creative productions of the local community. These may include poetry, music, dance, theater, and other forms of cultural and artistic expression.

Transformational action. Participants are committed to conscious action and social change using creative praxes and an engaged approach to policy that Valenzuela and López (2014) simply term "engaged policy" (Foley & Valenzuela, 2005; López, Valenzuela, & Garcia, 2011).

Concientización para la colectiva. This work is part of a movement, rather than discrete sets of isolated action. Goals include critical consciousness, social justice, and mutual liberation/emancipation from oppression.

GUIDING QUESTIONS AND PRACTICES

We offer the PAR principles as a developmental guide for consideration, rather than as a formula that presupposes a "standard" way of conducting PAR. However, we have come to understand that the principles do not stand alone. They are also built upon with guiding questions and various learning experiences that enrich the engagement that students, practitioners, and community members have with PAR. What follows are questions, examples, and activities tied to the PAR principles that inform and shape curriculum, pedagogy, and the research interests of those involved.

Principle: Participation

Questions

- Who is most impacted by the issue proposed for investigation? Why and how?
- Who should be at the table?
- In what ways can the collective build community as the group initially comes together?
- What process is the group using to make decisions?

There are two possible starting points for entering a participatory process:

1. The issue is already established and a community needs to be created.
2. The community is already established and defined and the issue has to be collectively determined.

Example 1: Graduation Standards. In *PAR Entremundos* (Ayala et al., forthcoming), one of the PAR examples describes a project focused on a state proposal to change graduation standards by adding a set of new requirements, including adding several standardized end-of-course exams. Although students (and teachers) are the ones likely to bear most of the impact of this kind of change, typically, they are not consulted about policy decisions. In this case, students were invited to participate in research on graduation standards, and also to engage in action that responded to the proposed change in standards.

Activity 1: Peer Invitations. Participation is an essential element for creating sustainable transformative action. If, as in the graduation standards example, young people are critical stakeholders, one way of encouraging engagement is to ask one or two students to gather a group of their peers to join with educators and community members in circles of conversation about the issue(s) of concern to them.

Example 2: Social Justice Education Project (SJEP). Students who enrolled in the SJEP formed a community of participants engaged in developing PAR projects. The students then formed smaller groups (five to eight students per group) that used particular generative themes to guide project work.

Activity 2: I Am Poetry. This activity begins with a process to develop themes connected to students' social and political realities. For instance, poetry with strong emotional content and language could be used to generate these themes. Facilitators provide a poetry template (I Am) and model the process. Then, participants in groups of no more than eight persons are invited to collectively produce their own words and prose related to their lived experiences (see Appendix K).

Principle: Critical Inquiry

Question

- What people, literature/readings, and/or media can the collective identify that offer a critical perspective on historical and current social and political issues?

Activity: Educational Dialogues. Educational dialogues can be used to engage students, providing opportunities to use theories of liberation and oppression and to think with a critical consciousness. For instance, one educational dialogue involved young people gathering to generate themes based on their personal schooling experiences—both empowering and disempowering ones. One student described his third-grade experience of language discrimination. Through dialogue, the group uncovered some underlying disempowering policies and practices. Another student shared her empowering experience with a sixth-grade teacher who supported and nurtured her vision of pursuing a college education. Her experience became the catalyst for discussions about social beliefs, behaviors, and common experiences across the collective.

Suggested Readings

Anzaldúa, G. (1987). *Borderlands/La Frontera: The new mestiza.* San Francisco, CA: Spinsters/Aunt Lute.

Ayala, J., Cammarota, J., Rivera, M., Rodríguez, L., Torre, M., & Berta-Ávila, M. (forthcoming). *PAR Entremundos: A pedagogy of the Américas.* New York, NY: Teachers College Press.

Cammarota, J., & Fine, M. (Eds.). (2008). *Revolutionizing education: Youth participatory action research in motion.* New York, NY: Routledge.

Delgado, R., & Stefancic, J. (Eds.). (1999). *Critical race theory: The cutting edge.* Philadelphia, PA: Temple University Press.

Fals-Borda, O., & Rahman, M. A. (1991). *Action and knowledge: Breaking the monopoly with participatory action research.* New York, NY: Apex Press.

Freire, P. (1970). *Pedagogy of the oppressed.* New York, NY: Continuum.

Irizarry, J. (2011). *The Latinization of U.S. schools: Successful teaching and learning in shifting cultural contexts.* Boulder, CO: Paradigm Publishers.

Park, P. (1999). People, knowledge, and change in participatory research. *Management Learning, 30*(2), 141–157.

Shor, I. (1993). Education is politics: Paulo Freire's critical pedagogy. In P. MacLaren & P. Leonard (Eds.), *Paulo Freire: A critical encounter.* New York, NY: Routledge.

Solórzano, D. G., & Yosso, T. J. (2002). Critical race methodology: Counter-storytelling as an analytical framework for education research. *Qualitative Inquiry, 8*(1), 23–44.

Torre, M. E. (2009). Participatory action research and critical race theory: Fueling spaces for *nos-otras* to research. *Urban Review, 41*(1), 106–120.

Torre, M. E., & Ayala J. (2009). Envisioning participatory action research *Entremundos. Feminism & Psychology, 19*(3), 387–393.

Principle: Knowledge Co-construction

Questions

- What are some important issues to address in the community? Why?
- How is this principle prioritized when we collect, analyze, interpret, and share data?
- How does knowledge co-construction emerge and cycle throughout the PAR process?

Example: Root Causes. In the first example presented in *PAR En-tremundos* (Ayala et al., forthcoming), symptoms and root causes of collectively defined issues were identified, and a PAR project was developed to address them. Specifically, dropping out of school, not attending classes, and performing poorly academically were identified as symptoms. Later, students named colonization as a root cause of discrimination, and then English-only policies were highlighted as practices sustaining the other symptoms of discrimination.

Activity 1: Dialogical Pedagogy—Why Do Students Drop Out of School? In the second PAR example presented in *PAR Entremundos* (Ayala et al., forthcoming), the PAR project participants used dialogical pedagogy to help them identify root causes of the dropout issue, moving from the personal to the collective and social. The same process can be applied to other issues. One way to make effective use of dialogical pedagogy is to start with a free-flowing session of brainstorming, recording participants' ideas on flipchart paper or a whiteboard. Then, participants should form small groups in which they can reflect on the generated list and begin to narrow down themes. Following this, they discuss and decide what emerged as the most significant issues across all the small groups. Narrowing that list to approximately five issues will give the group as a whole a manageable entry point for exploring key issues of collective concern. These dialogues can also become data.

Activity 2: Problem Tree. Once themes have been identified, they must be problematized. For instance, if equality is named as a theme, then the question is, "What is the problem form of equality?" An answer, such as discrimination, provides a starting point for inquiry. A problem tree is then jointly developed by taking the initial problem (trunk) and identifying symptoms (leaves and branches) and underlying causes (roots). A PAR project is designed to address policies and practices that sustain root causes.

For instance, using discrimination as the problem (trunk), the tree might include the following:

- *Branches/Leaves*: dropping out of school, not attending classes, performing poorly academically
- *Trunk*: discrimination
- *Roots*: colonization, systems of domination (racism, sexism, and others)

Principle: Power With(in)

Questions

- Where is each group member in the process?
- What steps is the collective taking to reflect on what is happening with the group throughout the project?
- How are group members' feelings and needs being taken into account as the collective tackles the difficult issues at hand?

Example 1: Political Autobiography. As Bartolomé (2008) has argued, to develop a foundation for critical engagement in and with communities, it is necessary to develop a sense of political and ideological clarity (also see Bartolomé & Balderrama, 2001). This exercise provides a space for participants to connect their current social and political awareness with formative moments or events that helped to shape their political identity. Participants are also encouraged to connect their political and ideological development with key ideas presented in the suggested readings (e.g., Freire's *Pedagogy of the Oppressed* [1970], listed in the earlier suggested readings, under the "Critical Inquiry" principle).

Activity 1: Political Autobiography. In this exercise, facilitators begin by sharing their personal and political narratives (these might include stories about schooling, family, or immigration, for example). Then, participants are invited to reflect on and write about personal relationships and experiences (struggles, insights) as a way of locating their individual stories (political, psychological, ideological, and intellectual narratives) within broader sociohistorical and political contexts and theories. This exercise provides all participants with an opportunity to dialogue and connect their *selves* with the concepts the group has read collectively.

Activity 2: Process Check. In any process, particularly when it is associated with a group (e.g., a high school or university class) or organization (PAR collective), it is imperative to engage in a series of process checks with the participants in order to assess individual participation and overall group development. These checks should be frequent (every 2–3 weeks) and may be done verbally and within a group format. However, some participants may not be comfortable sharing verbally or in front of the group. Another option is to have participants write answers to questions such as, "Where am I in the process?" and "What are my questions/concerns/fears/hopes?" Participants can then brainstorm about how best to share and process this information with the collective in order to better understand the group and its individual participants. This exercise can also be liberating for individuals who have not had the opportunity to share their inner feelings and perspectives about their experiences.

Example 2: Emotions Workshop. During part of the process at El Puente Academy for Peace and Justice (one of the PAR examples presented in *PAR Entremundos* [Ayala et al., forthcoming]), young people were guided through an emotions workshop in which readings on the science of emotions were assigned, neuroscience and psychology research was shared, and personal experiences were explored. The workshop also included practice with exercises designed to illuminate the physiological power of emotions, especially as related to our belief systems and behaviors (Damasio, 1999; LeDoux, 1998; Pert, 1997; Zull, 2002).

Activity 3: State Shifting. One of the exercises introduced during the emotions workshop was state shifting (Day, 2007), which involves participants first thinking about an emotionally charged situation, then writing down the story, listing the emotions experienced, and naming how the emotions felt in their bodies. Then, participants deliberately pause, engaging in deep breathing and heart-centered visualization. Finally, the emotionally charged situation is revisited from this relaxed and centered state of being, and new insights are chronicled.

Activity 4: Graffiti Walls. In the process of doing critical research work, information or situations arise that stir up strong feelings that need an outlet. Sometimes, young people do not feel comfortable verbalizing these emotions, may have trouble articulating them, or may express them in ways that are not productive to the group. Rather than ignore or suppress strong feelings, one strategy utilized by the Public Science Project (2012) is to offer "graffiti walls," places where people can write or draw their feelings about a particular issue in an uninhibited, safe way. Taping blank paper to the walls of a room and providing containers of crayons or markers is a simple way to create graffiti walls.

Facilitators can structure the use of the walls by offering prompts and a specific time in the day to do this: "Take a few minutes now to write or draw something that stood out to you today [or] something that you really disagreed with/made you mad." After the initial structured activity in which everyone participates, the graffiti wall is left up for the remainder of the group's time together. Then, at various points (typically during break times, but sometimes during an intense activity), members of the collective can return to the graffiti wall on their own to add other words or images. The group might also close the day's (or week's) activities with an informal debriefing, using the graffiti wall to set the agenda: Group members walk alongside the wall, reading and processing the words and images there, and then they have an opportunity to discuss, as a group, the activities and issues recorded on the wall. This gives each collective member an opportunity to process the feelings involved in doing critical research.

Principle: Indigenous Cosmologies

Questions

- How can individuals' physical, emotional, and spiritual ways of knowing—especially wisdom traditions—be incorporated into PAR work?
- How can healing rituals support activist efforts?
- In what ways has the southern tradition influenced current understandings of PAR in the United States?

Example: Recognizing Transhistorical Consciousness: The Role of Students. José Carlos Mariategui, a Peruvian political philosopher of the early 20th century, wrote about the significance of indigenous identities across the *Américas*. One of Mariategui's core essays on education appeared in his book *Seven Interpretive Essays of the Peruvian Reality* (1928/1971). This text references the International Congress of Students held in Mexico City in 1921. Two core demands were identified by students from across the *Américas*: Students should have a direct role or say in educational governance, and they should play a role in determining what and how content is taught. In today's educational context, students often have these same expectations, yet the U.S. school system seems to be constantly moving in a dramatically different direction. In what ways do students have a voice? How are they silenced? Keep in mind that voice can be vocal, physical, spiritual, or intellectual.

Activity 1: Mask Making. One integrated arts activity (drawn from another PAR example presented in *PAR Entremundos* [Ayala et al., forthcoming]) that a senior facilitator at El Puente Academy for Peace and Justice uses is mask making. The facilitator guides young people through a process of combining wisdom from their indigenous (e.g., Taíno) cultures (gleaned through reading, storytelling, and discussion) with the creation of art (such as papier-mâché, painting, and design). Mask making could be used in a PAR process to craft physical symbols of oppressive policies and practices, personal histories of trauma, or representations of desired and imagined identities. The masks also could be used in rituals and simple ceremonies created to burn away destructive patterns/systems, for example; or they can be used to celebrate new personal, collective ways of being.

Activity 2: Theatre of the Oppressed. Theater activities can be used to encourage PAR groups to embody different identities through role-play and sociodramas. For instance, Theatre of the Oppressed and Forum Theatre techniques (Boal, 1993) invite participants to use situations from their daily lives, animating them and allowing audience members to become actors in the scene. That is, "spectators become spect-actors," stopping the scene, becoming participants in the action, and, ultimately, informing the development of the personal, collective, and sociopolitical drama. As PAR group members try on different roles (e.g., of the oppressor, of an ancestor), new opportunities for healing, compassion (for self and others), and transformation emerge.

Activity 3: Movement Meditation. The art of movement provides another way for PAR participants to integrate embodied experiences. As biologists and neuroscientists affirm, the human brain works best when the body is in motion (Medina, 2008). PAR project concepts are often profoundly complex and emotional. Movement can help release the biopsychosocial tension and trauma that inevitably arise during PAR sessions, and may also nurture personal and collective healing. In addition, movement can open the possibility for authentic, creative vision work, where new ways of being in the world are imagined.

Some examples of movement from wisdom traditions include deep breathing, shaking, tapping, yoga, and free-form dance.

Principle: Creative Praxes

Questions

- How do (or could) the community's cultural arts inform the PAR process?
- Research is often seen as strictly logical and deductive. How can creative, imaginative, synthesizing activities be integrated into PAR work?
- How can creativity be incorporated into data collection and analysis?
- What are different ways the group can artfully express/communicate its message and findings to various audiences?
- How can opportunities for play as well as for work be incorporated into the PAR process?

Example 1: Informal Conversations and Play. To promote a common understanding of the research process for the New Jersey Urban Youth Research Initiative (NJUYRI), what Torre et al. (2008) term *research camps* were developed. These are day-long or overnight events that may involve undertaking intensive critical work, learning different ways of collecting data, analyzing information, constructing interview questions, coming up with action plans, and so forth. Because such work is often very intense, it makes sense to incorporate opportunities for downtime and informal play. Often, informal processing opportunities occur spontaneously in trains or buses while participants are on the way home from a session or presentation. In the NJUYRI example, two popular downtime activities were volleyball (the high school and adult researchers played together in games facilitated by members of the college volleyball team) and music and salsa dancing. Opportunities like these provide participants with other ways of seeing and interacting with each other. Play offers respite from the work, and it also can be another way to process the day's work and build community (Brown, 2010).

Example 2: Community Performance Theater. The Creative Justice Approach (CJA) is introduced in one of the PAR examples in *PAR*

Entremundos (Ayala et al., forthcoming). CJA is a conceptual framework for learning, rooted in creativity and social justice (Rivera et al., 2010). One way that El Puente (a community-based organization) and El Puente Academy for Peace and Justice (its public high school) implement the CJA is through integrated arts projects. In these projects, facilitators (or teachers) and young people engage in a critical and creative process to address current community issues through inquiry and action. In their academic classes, students learn about an issue (or issues) from multiple disciplinary perspectives (those of the humanities, physical, and social sciences, for example). Then, they engage these complex concepts through visual (painting, sculpting, mask making, collaging, photography), performing (theater, dance, music, spoken word/storytelling), and media arts (video/documentary making). Finally, a multi-arts community production is created and performed in neighborhood venues (local schools, gardens, community organizations, arts galleries) as an educational offering, sharing both what was learned and what action can be taken. Residents, activists, artists, and political representatives are invited to attend the performance and engage in dialogue about next steps.

Activity 1: Maps. Maps are integrated into PAR processes to elicit thoughts and emotion about an issue or area of inquiry using a creative medium. Given that human beings think in pictures that the brain then translates into words, encouraging El Puente and El Puente Academy for Peace and Justice research participants to share their dynamic and embodied insights, experiences, and feelings through art before engaging in the verbal dialogue of an interview enabled them to map whole concepts and journeys, creating a portal into rich conversation. Participants were given a prompt (for example, "map your learning experience at this school") and provided with paper, markers, crayons, scissors, and other materials to craft their maps. Participants then discussed their maps together, beginning a dialogue about the issue.

Activity 2: PhotoVoice. An alternative strategy that can be integrated into a PAR project is PhotoVoice. PhotoVoice offers an opportunity to utilize documentary photography to engage in a creative reflection process of naming the problem for inquiry, interpreting the problem from a personal standpoint, analyzing the problem using a macro lens, and, finally, engaging in creative transformative action that leads to community enhancement (Ada & Beutel, 1993). In this activity, the PAR facilitator/team invites participants to respond to guided questions by taking photos of images they feel represent experiences, realities, and understandings related to a specific guided question. The following three-part process has proven useful (Wang, Wu, Tao, & Carovano, 1998): (1) Begin by conducting two or three rounds of photo taking. After each round, ask participants to identify photos (possibly four or five) that most closely correlate with the research question(s). (2) Develop a narrative (in either written or oral form) that embodies the photos chosen. (3) Engage in a group dialogue with the PAR facilitator/team to determine the generative themes that emerge at an individual level and within a whole-group context.

Principle: Transformational Action

Questions

- What can be done about what was learned through the research?
- When should action(s) happen?
- Who needs to hear/know about what was learned?
- What is the best way to convey the message that needs to be heard?
- In what ways does a public presentation of the findings to key stakeholders serve as a transformative act? For whom and why?
- What are the broader policy implications of this work?

Example 1: Social Justice Education Project: Actions Taken by Students. The SJEP students created a video revealing the substandard conditions at their high school. The students distributed copies of the video to school board members, administrators, teachers, and other students. Two months after the release of the video, the principal began to invest money in the school to improve conditions, including repairing bathrooms, ceilings, and water fountains, and updating library materials and technology.

Activity 1: Demonstrating Expertise: Reflections on Past Experiences. Every day, students and teachers engage in transformative acts in the classroom. However, it is rare to find situations where these same students and teachers are given the opportunity to be public about their work. In this activity, PAR participants are encouraged to think of a moment when they were given the opportunity to demonstrate expertise, either as a student or teacher. What personal impact did this experience have? What impact did it have on others? Why?

Example 2: Community Report-Backs. The NJUYRI collective formed around a shared desire to take action on a changing educational policy. Thus, transformational action was part of the process during and after the research project. Multiple products and venues were used for dissemination, and because this was a multisite collective, local actions were taken independent of the collective's efforts. Members of one group, for instance, created their own video and staged a viewing in their local environment. Members of another group developed a workshop on the issue for middle school students in their community, and members of a third group made a presentation to their local board of education. The PAR team produced a policy report, based on survey and interview findings, and distributed it at the culminating collective presentation—that is, a community report-back session.

With an audience of 75 community organizers, officials from the state department of education (including the president of the State Board of Education), parents, educators, and college students and faculty, young and adult members of the collective jointly reported on the findings of the study. The presentation included a discussion of the research methods and analysis in addition to spoken-word performances, clips from the video documentary one group produced, and an invitation to the audience to participate in devising solutions. Reports were distributed alongside youth-created postcards emblazoned with slogans about the issue. Because the collective members, with their various community and political connections, were actively involved in creating the audience, the policy discussion following the presentation was a constructive one, in which community members and school board officials engaged in sometimes tense, but productive, dialogue.

Activity 2: Demonstrating Expertise: Presenting Research to a District School Board. Once data have been collected and findings are developed, members of the PAR collective can present their work to relevant stakeholders. The goal of the research should directly inform the purpose of the presentation, how it is framed, and the depth of the policy and practical recommendations that are presented. In some efforts, the collective could have had a particular audience in mind, only to learn through the research process that different audiences may be interested in the research and implications. Whether the audience for the research is predetermined or organically emerges based on the context and dynamics of the region, participants should use the findings to identify the most relevant audiences (e.g., school boards, city officials, policymakers, legislators, teachers, parents, youth, etc.). Participants can also determine if and when media and other public outlets for information distribution are useful and necessary. For instance, a research presentation to a school superintendent may warrant a particular message as he or she has a particular context in mind—the district, school board, students, and parents and community. On the other hand, another research presentation may address members of the school board, who have the same stakeholders in mind, but from a policy perspective. Yet, on an entirely different level, students may present their work to a room full of their peers. Thus, not only does audience help determine the nature of the presentation, but it also informs how the students frame their work and its implications, and helps determine what kind of publicity, if any, is needed to build momentum. Finally, it is vital that participants identify allies to support their work, especially if the findings are controversial or critical.

Principle: *Concientización para la Colectiva*/Conscientization for the Collective

Questions

- What do social justice and freedom mean to the individual participant? To the group as a whole?
- In what ways does a recognition of liberating/oppressing experiences serve to engage critical consciousness and encourage movement toward social justice goals?
- How have the actions of each individual informed the group's consciousness about particular issues? In what ways is the collective reflecting on the knowledge gained from engaging in specific actions?

- How can the collective's work be connected to and shared with others engaged in similar political projects (*intercambios*)?

Example: Caring Is a Constant. A PAR committee member offered these reflections on PAR work: "It is beautiful for me because I contribute to my community in a way that helps young people live healthy and productive lives. It is like gardening. It is wonderful for me because I can go into the community and witness beauty being cultivated, young lives blossoming. Even when the soil erodes or weeds and parasites threaten the garden, you continue to work because you feel responsible for the plant. Caring is not something you do intermittently; it is a constant. Thus, you work to revitalize the space. PAR is part of a movement."

Activity 1: Principles. Experiences that emerge from such activities as political autobiographies and educational dialogues become generative principles that guide the work and analysis of the PAR group. A facilitator would guide a reflective process that invites participants to synthesize individual and collective experiences and explore principles of transformation (both personal and social). Because PAR is a social movement, this process of reflection allows participants to see how local projects are connected to other regional, national, and global PAR initiatives.

Activity 2: PAR Gatherings. PAR gatherings of young people, community organizations, educators, and policymakers could be organized, virtually or in person, with different PAR collectives, possibly through the NLERAP regions (as well as nationally/globally). Such gatherings could become a space to share crosscutting efforts and to engage in movement building.

RESEARCH PROCESS

There is no standard approach or specific, step-by-step formula for conducting PAR. Yet, because the issue(s) and research question(s) are collectively identified, and because the PAR group collects and analyzes data to address the research question, it is imperative to use an iterative process that counters hegemonic modes of traditional research and aligns with the ontology and epistemology of PAR. Here, we divide the research process into three categories: (1) potential data-collection methods, (2) types of data analysis strategies, and (3) ways of sharing research findings. A list of associated strategies accompanies each category. This section closes with a brief description of the research process of one project, as an example.

Data-Collection Methods

- Surveys
- Interviews (structured, semistructured)
- Focus groups
- Meeting notes, archival documents
- Newspaper articles
- Artwork
- Visual art: maps, paintings, sketches, masks, photography (PhotoVoice)
- Performing arts: spoken word, songs, theater scripts, dance choreography
- Videos, documentaries
- Journals, blogs, Facebook posts, tweets
- Free-form writing
- Student-generated artifacts
- Participant observation (field notes)
- *Testimonios* and oral histories
- Policy analysis (e.g., comparing zero-tolerance policies across schools/districts)

Data Analyses and Interpretation[1]

- Coding analysis for generative themes
- Voice-centered analysis
- Interpretive poetics
- Survey analysis
- Statistics
- Grounded theory

Findings Dissemination

- Reports, essays, newspaper/journal articles, books
- Poetry and spoken-word performances
- Theater productions
- Gallery exhibitions
- Videos and documentaries
- Website development
- Policy briefs or memoranda
- Public presentations
- Court testimony

Research Process Example. In *PAR Entremundos* (Ayala et al., forthcoming), the NJUYRI example describes how developing a common framework for PAR took place in research camps addressing proposed changes by the state in students' graduation requirements. Once the research questions were identified, the intergenerational collective of high school youth researchers, community partners/educators, and university professors brainstormed in small groups about potential data-collection methods that could be used to respond to the guiding research question. The group decided on surveys, interviews, and equipment inventories (this meant inspecting their schools to identify, count, and examine the quality of lab equipment, classrooms, etc.). The data analysis was generally conducted in small intergenerational groups, although the university partners did some preparation beforehand. Numerical data, as well as text from open-ended sources, were included in the analysis. Tables with percentages and transcripts from open-ended survey data were prepared beforehand, along with some probing questions for each small group to discuss in the analysis and interpretation of findings. Also, there was a workshop on how to use Microsoft Excel and a brief introduction to SPSS statistical analysis software.

For the qualitative data, a sample set of analytic codes was created to provide starting points prior to the small-group work; the small groups then revised these codes (creating, deleting, recasting) and applied them to the transcripts. Had more time been available, it would have been preferable to create each code "from scratch" in these intergenerational groups, as well as to create the numeric tables with percentages, mean scores, and other descriptive statistics grouped together. The members of each small group documented their insights on flipchart paper and presented their analyses to the larger group. A large-group discussion of general findings and interpretations of what the smaller groups shared ended the analysis portion of the research camp.

NOTE

1. This is a simple list, not intended to be comprehensive, of potential data analysis strategies. For further information on some of these, see Gilligan, Brown, and Rogers (1988) and Rogers et al. (1999).

CHAPTER 5

Social Justice Education Project (SJEP)

A Case Example of PAR in a High School Classroom

Julio Cammarota

During the 2002–2003 school year, the Social Justice Education Project (SJEP) started at Cerro High School in Arizona's Tucson Unified School District (TUSD).[1] In only a few years, this specialized social science program had expanded to three other high schools (Campo, Pima, and Mountain). An aggregate of seven SJEP courses were offered every year in the TUSD. The students most likely to enroll in the SJEP were working-class Latinas and Latinos from the southwest area of the city, home to the highest concentration of Latinos. However, White, African American, and Native American students were also enrolled in the SJEP.

The SJEP program aligned with state-mandated history and U.S. government standards but at the same time involved students in youth participatory action research (YPAR) projects. During a year-long course, students earned all the social science credits they needed for graduation while they also learned graduate-level PAR techniques. YPAR requires every student to conduct an original qualitative research study. The students examine problems in their social and economic contexts and learn every step of the research process. Then, based on their research findings, they propose actions to solve the problems they have identified.

These YPAR projects focused on critical analyses of social justice problems and include presentations to parents and other members of the community, aimed at initiating change. Students learned qualitative research methods, most notably participant observation, for assessing and addressing the everyday injustices limiting their own and their peers' potential. Observations focused on aspects of the students' social context, which could include school, neighborhoods, and family. Students wrote up their observations in weekly field notes and sometimes conducted interviews with peers or teachers at their schools. They also utilized other qualitative, visual, or creative methods, such as photo and video documentation or theater. These creative praxes usually involved using innovative modes to present the evidence supporting key patterns they had identified in their field notes.

THE SELECTION OF RESEARCH THEMES

Students usually chose to investigate problems and issues that affect them personally. For example, they were allowed to select research themes from poems that they had written about that addressed problems they face in their social worlds. From a Freirean perspective, "'Words' are both a part of the 'world' and the means through which it is shaped and transformed" (Roberts, 1998, p. 110). The following poem, "Big Colorful Place," by Zulem Sonoqui[2] provides an example of a student poem that expresses words later employed to generate themes for investigation:

> I can't help but watch all these people interacting with each
>   other. Some just talk, other people fight with an anger so deep
>   that it fills their heads with rage;
> They seem unhappy. The people living unhappy lives know
>   what's going on, they know how it is to live in an unjust place;
> But I also notice one thing. I notice how some human beings
>   seem to think in their *pinche cabezas* ("crazy heads") that they
>   are higher than another human being, that they are of big
>   value and I notice how they spit in the face of these people
>   whose skin is red and burnt from the flames of the sun and
>   step on the hands that don't stop working, the ones that have
>   blisters and their skin so rough and peely;
> I hear the yells, I hear the altercations and the sayings;
> They talk about society and illegal aliens coming in left and right
>   to a whites only place;

We all know who they call illegal aliens, but would they call a
    person from Europe an alien?
I listen to all this bullshit, and I just think to myself, "Why?"
They express it in the way of whoever doesn't have their color,
    falls beneath their shoes;
I think of just knocking the "shit" out of them with the power
    that has been building up more and more, and asking how
    does it feel to be down there;
They imagine that people like me are trouble, and we evolved
    just to serve them;
But I try to believe and think positive;
We know there's a lot of people out there, with this attitude, so
    what do I do?
There's only the way to think outside the premises and say
    something!

Students collectively identify the poignant generative themes wo-
ven throughout one another's poems. In "Big Colorful Place," students
identified themes of racism, discrimination, immigration, and political movements. Identifying generative themes, including words from
poetry, derives from Freire's (1993, 1994, 1998) critical literacy approach. Critical literacy facilitates students' production of new meanings and ideas that counter dominant, hegemonic messages, myths,
and beliefs designed to perpetuate subordination (Renner, Brown,
Steins, & Burton, 2010). "A 'generative theme' is a theme that elic-
its interest from the participants because it is drawn from their lives"
(Peckham, 2003, p. 231). Themes are relevant and speak to the social,
political, and economic conditions of students. Generative themes are
not new. Educators have employed them for critical and transformative learning processes in a variety of educational areas and subjects,
including, for example, special needs, bilingual education, math, and
service learning (Gent, 2009; Goldstein, 1995; Gutstein, 2006).

Students begin the SJEP process by conducting research observations of their own lived context. This, in accordance with the Freirean
literacy approach, is a preliminary step preceding the development of
generative themes (Barndt, 1998). The students use their observations
as a source for creating poetry. The students then work collectively to
identify generative themes in the poems.

Freire recommends that "researchers" or "investigators," apart
from the students, should conduct the observations (Roberts, 1994).

However, in the SJEP, students are the researchers who identify the poignant words that are germane to their own lived contexts. This ensures the selection of themes with the greatest relevance to their lives. For instance, in the poetry example described earlier, a group of five students identified the topic of "discrimination." They agreed with the poem's author that some people treat Latinos unfairly. This topic could lead to many other themes—language oppression, anti-immigration laws, curricular tracking, or suspensions—that suggest how institutional policies instigate the problem of mistreatment.

PROBLEMATIZING THEMES

Once students select generative themes, the process moves to problematizing to ensure that symptoms of problems attributed in generative themes are not mistaken for root causes. Students learn that focusing on symptoms will only lead to a superficial and ineffective understanding of the problem because the root causes will remain unchallenged and unchanged. For instance, if students select the generative theme of racially or ethnically based curricular tracking for investigation, they need to come to understand that both dropping out and segregation reflect symptoms of the problem and not the root cause.

In the poetry example, once discrimination was identified as a generative theme, the five students moved through a process in which they listed symptoms prior to understanding the root causes. Symptoms of discrimination may include disengagement, absenteeism, low achievement, or failure. After identifying symptoms, students began to discuss and identify root causes, noting how power, colonization, and racism represented the foundation or "roots" of problems related to discriminatory or unfair treatment. Once the students identified the roots, they began looking for solutions by discussing, first, how specific processes and practices influence or contribute to maintaining root causes in their own social environments. For example, regarding discrimination, students pointed to educational policies and practices, such as English-only strategies or ability-grouping programs (tracking), that continue to sustain the roots of power, colonization, and racism.

After students completed problematizing discrimination, they determined the focus of their YPAR projects. They decided that because several of them had direct experience with discriminatory treatment in their English language development (ELD) classes, that very program would be appropriate as a research focus.

Once that decision was made, the five students formed a project group and focused their research on cultural/language discrimination at school. They found that in the ELD program, students' greater understanding of Spanish than of English prompted conflicts with their teachers. For example, when students could not adequately articulate their thoughts or comments in English and thus resorted to Spanish, teachers would frequently punish them. Punishments took the form of extra assignments, after-school detention, or verbal humiliation. Members of the language/cultural discrimination group documented these interactions to demonstrate the colonizing approach embedded in the teaching practices of ELD programs.

COLLECTING DATA

The primary method for documenting school experiences consisted of participant observation and the writing up of field notes. Students were asked to conduct observations of their day-to-day school lives through the Freirean lens of "reading the world." This approach helped them to understand Freire's critical literacy approach. When students placed their emphasis on capturing the social practices and processes that accompanied their interactions with teachers and other students, they learned how to both be attentive to and document the external forces bearing on their social relationships.

This orientation of capturing the social influences on one's existence requires what Freire calls *conscientization*. A student who attains conscientization no longer views persistent social and economic obstacles (e.g., lack of resources or opportunities) as an internal problem with the self but rather sees the problem as deriving from external factors (policies and practices) initiated by others. Conscientization allows individuals to stop blaming themselves for negative experiences and outcomes, and simultaneously promotes recognition of the ways in which others' actions (or lack of actions) may present barriers to the accomplishment of goals. Thus, changing one's existence involves addressing conflicts in social relationships and attuning oneself to internal capabilities to produce transformation.

The attainment of conscientization requires a deep commitment to the observation of life's circumstances in order to understand how social practices and processes either facilitate or diminish human potential. Conducting observations with conscientization leads to two important discoveries. First, students will notice how daily external pressures impede forward progress and the attainment of success. Second, students will become empowered and realize that they have the potential to excel despite other people's deleterious judgments. These are interconnected discoveries that manifest themselves only when students focus their observations on the social practices and processes that impede progress and therefore must be changed to improve their educational experiences. By focusing on social impediments, students recognize that despite the many ways that their sense of self has been diminished, they actually do possess advanced cognitive capabilities. Then, as they embark on intellectualizing and theorizing, they learn the actions necessary to engender much-needed changes in their respective worlds.

Conducting participant observation that leads to the dual discoveries of social impediments and personal capabilities is what Freire might define as praxis: critical reflection and action. Praxis involves reflecting or "observing" a situation and then understanding the changes necessary to improve conditions within that situation. The only way to properly identify the required change is to initiate actions that result in improved circumstances. From these actions, new knowledge illuminates how the structure and content of situations are contingent upon value-laden preferences and exigencies. The inevitable epiphany emerging from this new knowledge is that alternative and just human contributions will produce better and more equitable conditions.

Because students must provide a detailed reflection about a situation and must write down their thoughts about how to initiate improvements, observations and field notes constitute praxis. Subsequently, the participant observation method generates new knowledge on how to act to ameliorate conditions. Praxis embedded in the students' participant observation provides details of the site in question and a strong commitment to write about an approach that will engender greater justice. Action occurs through this commitment to put in writing the words that theorize new possibilities and practices of learning. In the following section, raw observational data taken from the language/cultural discrimination group's field notes has been put into narrative form to allow a better understanding of the meaning and context of the situation under discussion. The praxis represented by the students' field notes demonstrates their conscientization and their drive for social justice.

STUDENT OBSERVATIONAL DATA

One student, Zury González, documents in her notes how a teacher who misinterpreted policies around language and education told her that she should not speak Spanish.[3] In her freshman year, Zury was incapable of communicating or writing in English and would often rely on Spanish to communicate with peers to understand course material. The teacher decided to punish Zury for speaking Spanish by assigning her to write a paper on the topic of "Why We Shouldn't Talk Spanish in Class." She attempted to write the paper but had difficulty doing so in the English language. Her limited ability in English prevented her from completing the assignment, so the teacher decided to punish her with after-school detention. She writes that she was not a special case and that many of her fellow English language learner (ELL) students received detention for speaking Spanish.

These students started to make an erroneous connection between speaking Spanish and having disciplinary problems. In addition, students started to feel traumatized when they were punished for speaking Spanish. Zury reports that many of her ELL classmates started to internalize the belief that because they spoke Spanish, they were a "problem" or were delinquent students. The unintended consequence of punishing students for speaking Spanish is that these students adopted the belief that there is something wrong with them, and that they are not well-adapted, normal students. Students with this mindset are likely to disengage, become marginalized, and feel incapable of learning.

Being reprimanded for speaking Spanish is a common occurrence in Arizona schools. Recounting a situation similar to the one Zury describes, another student, Amanda López, writes about a friend, Leticia, who was told by a teacher not to speak Spanish in algebra class. The teacher incorrectly cited language policy and demanded that students speak only English. Amanda states that Leticia did not speak English, and when she attempted to communicate with Amanda in Spanish, the teacher scolded Leticia in front of her classmates. This public humiliation thwarted Leticia's language development by making her feel uncomfortable communicating in any language.

Humberto Cárdenas writes about how his teacher punished him and other students for speaking Spanish in an ELD class. He explains how his teacher would write on the board the names of students who spoke Spanish during class. A check mark next to a name signified a day in detention. Students "caught" speaking Spanish more than once might have several check marks next to their names. Humberto also mentions how the teacher would become angry with these individuals and yell at them for speaking Spanish.

The English-only discourse translates into a hierarchy in which certain students believe that they are superior and thus more entitled than others. SJEP student Lisette Montoya writes in her field notes about a language conflict between students in her English class. The conflict reveals how certain English-dominant students saw themselves as superior, which then led them to believe the school should cater to their cultural and linguistic orientation. The incident, Lisette reports, happened after school announcements (made over the public announcement system) had been completed. The announcements were given in both English and Spanish—English first, then Spanish immediately after. When the Spanish announcements were completed, one student shouted, "How ghetto!" Lisette states that one girl yelled, "Speak English," while another added, "We're in America." A Latina student angrily stated, "Well, look around—the majority at this school are Hispanics." A White student responded by saying, "I speak English, so everyone else should, too. We're in America."

The actions of the anti-Latino students appeared to be an attempt to maintain their dominance over the majority at the school. Although the school's demographics were rapidly changing in the opposite direction, White students wanted to sustain the dominance of English at the school and thus keep their advantage. However, becoming a White minority does not mean that these students would lose their power and status. An apartheid structure is a present and unfortunate reality. By maintaining English as the dominant language, these students continued to hold onto and argue for their cultural superiority, despite their diminishing percentage of the school population.

At this same school, student Martín Portugal observes that many students made remarks like "shut up and go back to your country, *mojado*," or called people "illegal aliens," even when the person saying it was of the same race (i.e., Hispanic/Mexican/Latino). Latinos often adopt an internalize racist discourse because it permeates and saturates their sociocultural context. These kinds of racist remarks, heard every day, enter students' heads, blocking their own perspectives and communication (see Valenzuela [2008] for a cogent analysis of internalized racism).

Martín also writes about conversations where he heard other students saying, "Students that were born here have to share their school with students from all over the world, and they don't believe it's fair that these students get opportunities that they were not allowed to get." This "loss-of-privilege" discourse, Martín notes, derives from the belief that certain students, in this case Anglo students, experience the disadvantage of not receiving "special" treatment. Because they do not receive special treatment, they are supposedly missing out on vital opportunities. These Anglo students fail to recognize that as Whites, they have the privilege of an entire school and curriculum that has been tailored to promote their success. Arguing against opportunities for students of color by invoking power-evasive notions of "fairness" allows Anglo students to rationalize and maintain their own privileges. If students of color have advantages, then Anglo students can argue and feel justified about holding onto their own privileges.

Students who speak Spanish experience a disadvantage with language policy at school. ELL students must spend most of their time at school learning English, even foregoing other coursework necessary for graduation. Zury González comments about ELL students' scheduling problems. Because they are scheduled primarily for English classes, they do not have time for math, science, or history. When they reach their senior year, many ELL students lack the credits they need for graduation. The only option at this point is to take weekend academy or summer courses. English requirements for ELL students impose serious obstacles to timely graduation.

ANALYSIS AND PRESENTATION

After SJEP students conduct observations and write their field notes, they initiate analyses that involve identifying the relevant patterns in the data. Excerpts from field notes that reflect those patterns are organized and placed within an analytical category called a *code*. Each code is a term that the students create to reference the general meaning behind the pattern(s) that they identify in their field notes. For instance, the students organized the field note data presented in the previous section into a code they termed the "Spanish Disadvantage."

The relatively high frequency with which students were reprimanded for speaking Spanish led to the interpretation that the students' use of Spanish made them feel disadvantaged at school. Spanish had no other purpose than allowing certain teachers and students to label Spanish speakers as delinquent or deficient. Thus, speaking Spanish had the unfortunate consequence of placing ELL students at a disadvantage across the whole curriculum and compromised their ability to become literate in any language.

The coding analysis of the YPAR process spurs students' creativity and imagination. They must reflect on the data and then create new terms (codes) that relate to the experiences documented in field notes. Frequently, students amass enough data to generate several codes. The codes they create often are striking in their combination of originality and accuracy. For instance, the students who created the "Spanish Disadvantage" code also invented a code called "English Submersion" to indicate how English requirements hold students down by taking away the time needed to meet other requirements (coursework in math, science, history) for graduation. "English Submersion" is also an imaginative play on words because the name for the teaching approach used in ELD classes is structured English immersion (SEI). By switching *submersion* for *immersion*, students suggest that the SEI approach actually submerges students as opposed to uplifting them.

Students not only create codes or new terms from the data but also look to creative praxes to present them. After students create codes, they delve deep within their imaginations to conceive of an original representation of the new term. With the "Spanish Disadvantage," students created a role-playing skit from the supporting field note data. The skit retold the racist incident with the bilingual announcements mentioned earlier. They wrote out the dialogue from the incident, including roles for the announcer, Latina students, and Anglo students. Every time they presented their research, the students would define the "Spanish Disadvantage" and then hand out cards with the different roles and dialogue. The skit would reenact the bilingual announcement incident, pulling the dialogue directly from their field notes. The audience experienced a physical representation of the research in the form of drama. This creative presentation also allowed some audience members to adopt roles and participate in the reenactment while others witnessed the embodiment of the incident through live human action and expression. Because the skit connects people directly to the meaning and experience of the "Spanish Disadvantage," it gives them a sense, in a dramatic way, of how disadvantaged students may feel.

After students conduct the skit, they lead the audience in a dialogue about the "Spanish Disadvantage." The students initiate dialogue by eliciting the audience's general thoughts about the skit, and about how this racist incident could be used for a "teachable moment" in the classroom. They also pose direct questions to those involved in the role-playing, asking them how they felt reenacting the incident. The intention of the dialogue is to foster a praxis in which reflection on the situation is coupled with the action of drama. The creative expressions of theater allow people to not only think about discrimination but also to act out a situation that provokes discriminatory practices. In that sense, knowledge produced through reflection and action or praxis evinces the causes of the problems. It is through this understanding of how problems are produced that knowledge emerges to suggest how changes may occur. By understanding the root causes behind the problem (e.g., language discrimination), people can develop strategies, such as pro-Spanish discourse, to challenge these causes.

ENCUENTROS: THE FINAL PRODUCTION OF PRAXIS

At the end of the year, the students present their research at a parent and student meeting organized by the SJEP. This *Encuentro* represents the culmination of the students' work as well as of the full cycle of YPAR. The *Encuentro* is based on theories of learning situated in the process of dialogue and the formative potential of tightening social bonds. At the beginning of the year, the students read Freire (1993). At the end of the year, they put into practice the knowledge they had built through their research into the students' and the community's social experiences of marginalization and injustice.

In the SJEP, families are not perceived to exist "as deficit." The SJEP follows the approach of "funds of knowledge" (González, 1995; González, Moll, & Amanti, 2005; Moll, González, Amanti, & Neff, 1992), which recognizes families' cultivation of novel cultural practices as these become necessary for their survival and advancement. These cultural practices bear sophisticated intellectual content that helps families negotiate the many challenges of a penurious existence. Yet, schools often ignore students' funds of knowledge. Through *Encuentros*, the SJEP, in contrast, deliberately draws on this kind of "community cultural wealth" (Yosso, 2005) to dialogue about the injustices facing Latinos in education. The SJEP holds several *Encuentros* throughout the year; in each one, families discuss the funds of knowledge—or inherent cultural wealth—that mediate their children's learning.

Encuentros represent true funds of knowledge: Transformation occurs with students, as well as their families. Students, through their actualization as public intellectuals, see themselves as knowledgeable. This in turn solidifies their academic identities. Family members discover that SJEP students act on their behalf by producing new funds of knowledge that might create better opportunities for them and their communities. Buy-in and support for the SJEP has grown considerably over the past few years because of the now prevalent belief among families that the experience of participating in the program will itself improve academic and social outcomes for Tucson's Latinos/as.[4]

At the *Encuentro*, members of the language/cultural discrimination group presented their YPAR work in the form of their drama/skit "Spanish Disadvantage," followed by a facilitated discussion with parents and community members. In discussing the fact that some school officials tell students they may not speak in any language other than English, the students pointed out that the state's anti-bilingual law restricts *teachers*, not students, from speaking languages other than English (during instruction). Thus, the law does not prohibit students from speaking Spanish or other non-English languages. Such a provision would violate students' First Amendment right to freedom of speech.

Students skillfully presented evidence of teachers and security monitors who forbid them to speak Spanish, as well as laws on language and speech rights, to demonstrate how teachers and other school personnel violate their rights daily. After hearing the students' follow-up to their "Spanish Disadvantage skit," one parent stood up and said that this unjust practice was happening at his workplace. His boss would often tell him and his coworkers that they could not speak Spanish. Now, after hearing his son explain about language rights, this parent said that he would stand up to his boss and find out why Spanish is prohibited.

Encuentros give students the opportunity to participate in critical reading and engagement. This allows them to generate funds of knowledge that solidify their academic identities among themselves and also influence new possibilities for change among their families and communities. The students' adoption of intellectual status invariably results in epiphanies among those who engage with, and listen to, them. Their presentations reveal the sense that they are acting in the best interest of others.

CONCLUSION

The work done by the language/cultural discrimination group shows how learning a language through punishment, humiliation, and repetition works against Freire's theory for an effective literacy approach. In contrast, Freire's approach involves grounding words and language in the learner's sociopolitical context. Recent research has shown how involving students in real-life discussions and analysis of race, gender, class, culture, and power provides an effective pedagogical strategy for language development (e.g., Goldstein, 1995; also see "Topic 6: Language, Literacy and Culture" in Chapter 3 of this volume). An effective literacy for ELL students should therefore include an examination of language policies and the ways in which the design of current ELD programs prevents students from acquiring proficiency in any language. Contemplating and discussing labels, including *English as Second Language (ESL), ELD,* and *ELL,* could foster generative themes that would encourage students to focus more closely on language policies that negatively influence their learning, a first step in overcoming these barriers. Jon Austin and Andrew Hickey (2008) assert that

> transformative education requires authentic knowledge of, and connection with, the experiences, histories, and hopes of those who inhabit the margins. By this we suggest that educators must give voice to those whose stories are typically unheard while at the same time opening for critique the dominant hegemonic narratives that would continue the silencing process. (p. 135)

An education that is focused on the role of power in learning would itself be an empowering and transformative process for marginalized students.

The examination of generative themes in educational policy is the praxis strategy for the SJEP. By analyzing their own educational experiences; noticing how school policies, either formal or informal, have determined the form and content of their learning process; and further noticing how some policies can be detrimental, students begin to understand that failure is no fault of their own, but rather that it is manufactured by others who secure, by design, advantages for some at the expense of others. Recognizing how policies construct artificial barriers involves grasping the "limit situation" of the institutional structure. Limit situations are "limits that—once recognized as constructed rather than natural or determined—can be acted upon and deconstructed or transformed" (Klein, 2007, p. 191). These actions include recognizing the social impediments to success, ignoring the deficit discourses utilized to rationalize explicit disadvantages, and embracing funds of knowledge to initiate change. Once the SJEP students engage in these actions, they experience increased self-confidence that moves them beyond feelings of inadequacy to a sense of competence and mastery. They realize they can learn, and learn in ways that not only better themselves but that also improve circumstances in education so that others may succeed, as well.

This PAR case example illustrates many of the practices and principles described in the PAR Practitioner's Guide (Chapter 4), such as the use of generative themes, ways to problematize root causes, and approaches to transformational action. See Appendix K for a brief guide to implementing a PAR process; Appendix K, which is based on this SJEP example, summarizes key phases and provides suggestions for activities to accompany each phase.

NOTES

1. This chapter was written prior to the ethnic studies ban in the Tucson Unified School District that effectively shut down the project. However, it re-started in 2014 under the name Culturally Responsive Curriculum. This new project is currently offered at one high school in the Tucson Unified School District.

2. The names of the students and schools have been changed to pseudonyms to maintain confidentiality.

3. In 2000, Arizona voters passed Proposition 203, which effectively banned bilingual education in the state. The law mandates that English must be the only language of instruction in all primary subjects as well as English language development (ELD) programs. Nowhere in this law does it state that students cannot speak languages other than English. It is the teacher who is prevented from speaking different languages, not the students.

4. The Arizona Department of Education contracted the Cambium Learning Group to evaluate the SJEP and the entire MAS program (see Cambium
Learning, 2004). The final evaluation in the Cambium report indicates that
MAS met its goal of improving academic outcomes for students of color. For
a summary of the report, please follow this link: http://www.acluaz.org/sites/
default/files/documents/Ethnic%20studies%20audit%20summary.pdf

CHAPTER 6

Conclusion: *El Árbol*/The Tree
Returning to the Root

Angela Valenzuela

It is hard to bring a volume like this to a close. It was written in the interstices of our busy lives where we, as researchers, teachers, and community-engaged scholars and members of community-based organizations, have nevertheless collaborated extensively to develop this curriculum for higher education teacher preparation in the context of the National Latino/a Education Research and Policy Project's (NLERAP's) Grow Your Own Teacher Education Institutes (GYO-TEI) initiative. Ours is a deep and defining commitment to equity, social justice, and a more beautiful world that centers community, teachers, teaching, and teacher preparation as essential parts of the solution to the deep sense of alienation that so many of our children and teachers experience in our nation's schools.

In *Beyond Alienation: A Philosophy of Education for the Crisis of Democracy,* the late Nobel Laureate Ernest Becker (1967) states that humans are the "one animal in nature who, *par excellence*, lives and thrives on the creation of meaning" (p. 198). Tragically, Becker maintains, as much as we breathe and process symbols and symbolic meanings, we have been "instinctivized" to follow the herd, and we consequently fear our own meanings, thoughts, and intuition that come from our creative depths. To this, Becker (1967) adds that schools must teach what part each individual is to play, with his or her own free energies, "in furthering the life pulse of the universe itself" (p. 211).

With both the "pulse of the universe" and the creation of new meanings of the good, the true, and the beautiful in mind, this handbook opens with the metaphor of *El Árbol*, which seems a fitting way to conclude. Among other things, *El Árbol* invokes a generational consciousness—or ancestral form of accountability—that is encrypted, available for decoding, so that we might acquire a sense of meaning, purpose, and direction in our pursuit of freedom for all of humanity in a world that seems to be spinning out of control.

In this vein, Carmen Tafolla (2014), State of Texas Poet Laureate for 2015, offers us this poem titled "Our *Abuelos*, the Trees" ("Our Grandparents, the Trees") that helps us to circle back to *El Árbol*, NLERAP's guiding metaphor:

> Our Abuelos, the trees, stand guard,
> Their bark-lidded eyes, tired from too much wisdom,
> have seen a thing or two.
> They sometimes sit so still
> we don't even see them
> Always, they see us
> squint those wooden curandero eyes
> at foolish grandchildren so so
> young they think that they
> discovered this place
> discovered history
> discovered life.
> Los Abuelos laugh among themselves
> shake their heads, leaves tossed like greying locks
> tremble in a deep breath
> settled in for a another siglo [century] or two
> and hope the grand children
> won't tear up the place too much in the meanwhile
> Our Abuelos, the trees, hung low lullabies around us
> whisper words of warning beside us
> hope we'll eventually grow up enough
> to learn to speak the language
> or at least learn how to behave
> when spoken to (p. 34)

We have much to learn from our *abuelos* and *antepasados*, or grandparents and ancestors, respectively. As the poem states, our *abuelos* sit so very still that they are scarcely audible or visible despite their presence as enduring figures in our lives—and the lives of many generations before us. If only we would stop to notice them, we might see how their squinted *curandero* (healing) eyes and their weather-worn expressions speak volumes and bring wisdom and healing. They want us to be as close to the ground in our identities as possible—to be real people, singing and dancing and making real changes in the world, dedicating our time, strengths, and talents in the service of others and for the common good. They do this, in part, by calling our attention to the protective presence of their shade, experienced as comforting and consoling "lullabies," as well as through the whispered "words of warning" when we have lost our way.

The protective power of *El Árbol* is captured well by renowned Chicana feminist and community advocate and elder, Martha P. Cotera, who once shared this *dicho* (saying) with me in a conversation we had about how our political identities are formed across the generations (Valenzuela, 2012): *"Al que a buen árbol se arrima, buena sombra le cobija"* ("If we get close to a good tree, a good shade covers us"). This is a statement about mentorship: We never bask in a mentor's shadow, but rather in the mentor's shade. Mentorship, as well as all educational experiences, generally, should be nurturing and fulfilling.

El Árbol commands our deepest respect: It wants us to listen humbly to the reverberations of the awesome whole of creation that breathes through the *árboles*. *Árboles viejos*, old trees, have not only survived and endured the test of time, but they have a message for the *siglos*, the ages. They urge us to engage "place," "history," and "life," making our lives, at their best, an organic, fulfilling, community-based journey, rooted in a strong sense of purpose to bring about—*through la buena educación*—our shared dreams, hopes, and desires for present and future generations. What narrative will our great-grandchildren, great-grandnieces and great-grandnephews—indeed, all of our kin—tell about how their great-grandparents conducted themselves in the face of senseless and brutal wars, unspeakable violence, genocidal campaigns, or the constant impending threat of ecocide and biocide?

To carry on this great task of educating our youth, we need the wisdom of our elders. We need them to help us recover and apprehend this ancestral memory of their powerful, enduring presence, as well as their "whisper[ed] words of warning," that issue from the innermost depths of our being. These are the intangibles of the unconscious—that unshakeable desire, unspoken calling, and deep yearning for social justice to make things right—that inhabit our "underground" in the almost inaccessible, deeply rooted structures of historic and continuing trauma, sacrifice, and suffering. Despite *El Ábrol's*, heavy "bark-lidded eyes, tired from too much wisdom," our psyches and souls bear a heavy burden and responsibility, even if largely unbeknownst to us at a conscious, everyday level.

This ancestral warning or admonition is to not get caught up too much in the mundane, lest we fail to hear that subtle, stirring, and life-saving call to consciousness, to use our privilege as educators and leaders to foster through all that we do the creation of new meanings and new individual aesthetics of the good, the true, and the beautiful (Becker, 1967). According to Becker (1967) and the late, distinguished philosopher and beloved professor Maxine Greene (1998), the way that this gets done is by capitalizing on the universal appeal of freedom that our curriculum handbook— through its many sources, frameworks, readings, and activities— hopes to inspire.

As well expressed by Greene (1998), our society and educational system advance ways of knowing and achieving freedom in the world that promote individualistic, consumeristic, and privatized identities, in which "freedom" often extends little beyond personal and limited notions of gain. Moreover, these narrow notions of profit and gain deprive us of a full awareness of who we are and what we can become. If we are not critically reflective, we may opt for *having*, rather than *being*, more. In so doing, we risk becoming unwitting conspirators in the diminishment of our own power, and thusly, our sense of selves. A diminished sense of self both serves the interests of current constellations of power and robs us of a conscious awareness not only of our personal and individual possibilities, but also the enormous potential that is literally within our grasp to transform our schools and communities in all the ways that we envision.

Finally, as a collective of community advocates, researchers, university faculty, and published scholars, we, in the National Latino/a Education Research and Policy Project, exercise our privilege and autonomy as meaning makers to share our wisdom, knowledge, and experiences together with insights into our action- and place-based pedagogy that are embodied in this handbook and *PAR Entremundos* (Ayala et al., forthcoming). These contributions, themselves the progeny of personal and professional struggle, are intended to reach people far beyond our own brief sojourn on this Earth. We are humbled by the thought that the important task of pulling this volume together is so much bigger, deeper, and more beautiful than any of us could have anticipated at the onset. *Los Árboles*, our ancestors, would not have had it otherwise.

Afterword

Growing Critically Conscious Teachers excites me because the initiative it presents, and the larger system of roots in which the initiative is grounded, synthesize what are often disparate considerations of what students of color need from teachers, and how those teachers should be prepared. We have studies reporting what Latino/a students say matters most to them in their teachers (e.g., Franquiz & Salazar, 2004), studies of Latino/a household funds of knowledge (Moll, González, Amanti, & Neff, 1992), studies of Latino/a teachers (e.g., Ochoa, 2007), and studies of projects to recruit and prepare Latino/a teachers (e.g., Flores, Clark, Claeys, & Villareal, 2007), but few works that bring these and other strands together. Adding to disjointedness, teaching itself takes place in schools, while traditional teacher preparation takes place largely in universities, usually and at best with only cursory linkages to students' communities.

I recognize a kind of separateness of these areas in my own work. One strand of my work has involved teaching teacher candidates how to engage with and learn from communities in which they teach. Recognizing the need to connect teaching with students' cultural and experiential lives, I worked for years with community-based organizations to design field experiences so that my teacher candidates would learn to recognize and capitalize on local funds of knowledge (Boyle-Baise & Sleeter, 2000). A related strand involved grounding my teacher education courses in sociocultural and sociopolitical theory and praxis. But since most teacher candidates in those courses were White, I ended up investing considerable energy trying to figure out how to cultivate justice-oriented commitments in candidates who did not go into teaching to become social justice teachers (Sleeter, 2008). Yet another strand of work has involved diversifying the teacher workforce. After briefly working in a grow your own program many years ago, and learning how racism maintains a predominantly White teacher force, I have

collaborated with colleagues to address this issue (Sleeter, Neal, &
Kumashiro, 2015).

Growing Critically Conscious Teachers puts these pieces together. This
book reflects on a holistic and sustaining model that links teacher recruitment, teacher preparation, and classroom pedagogy for Latino/a
students. The model places the education of children and youth of
color, and the preparation of teachers of color, in the same book, the
same paragraph, the same breath, rather than in separate books and
separate institutions. Indeed, the two signature courses can be adapted
for multiple levels of education, ranging from secondary school
through teacher preparation. At the secondary level, the courses prepare youth to claim an intellectual self, rooted in their own ethnic
identity and responsive to issues in their communities. The curriculum prepares them to continue with their education, thereby creating
a pipeline of Latino/a youth who may become future teachers. At the
teacher preparation level, the courses prepare teachers who, through
their engagement with students, families, and communities, become
effective teachers who are *change* rather than *changed* (Achinstein &
Ogawa, 2011), agents.

The signature courses prepare teachers and youth not only *for*
communities of color, but also as collaborators *with* communities, very
much in the spirit of the late Peter C. Murrell, who worked extensively
to prepare "community teachers." According to Murrell (2001), a community teacher "actively researches the knowledge traditions of the
cultures represented among the children, families, and communities
he or she serves" and "enacts those knowledge traditions as a means
of making meaningful connections for and with the children and their
families" (p. 54). Like the African symbol Sankofa, which represents
drawing from the past to create the future, the NLERAP model em-
braces the knowledge of familial and community elders. Education is
conceived not as a process of replacing accumulated community knowledge with school knowledge, but rather as leveraging both in ways
that support collective intellectual, cultural, and spiritual well-being.
As the signature courses make clear, the education process is relational
rather than individualistic; it is intellectual, and it is "agentic."

Adding to the sustaining and transformational nature of the curriculum is its infrastructure support. Most programs designed to recruit
and prepare teachers of color are very small and most last only a few
years. In contrast, the NLERAP initiative is supported by a preexisting national office as well as a nonprofit that raises funds. This means

that affiliated programs can focus their energies on the program itself, rather than on the program's survival, and those working in affiliated programs have a network of colleagues around the country they can call on. I am very optimistic that this network, nested within a sustaining infrastructure, will lead to the longevity and strength of affiliated programs.

NLERAP is part of a research agenda on Latino/a education, and I believe that a well-crafted research agenda will be critically important. Two things we learn from Tucson's experience with ethnic studies are that (1) fierce political backlash must be anticipated in response to any program that produces academically strong and politically active youth and teachers of color; and (2) rigorous research, including statistical research using prevailing measures of education success, can be a significant tool for fighting back. In Tucson, largely because of a rigorous statistical study (Cabrera, Milem, Jaquette, & Marx, 2014) and Tucson's desegregation status, ethnic studies have been revived under a different name (culturally relevant curriculum and pedagogy). Without the research, the revival probably would not have happened. Not only will NLERAP's research findings be welcome to those of us who have been working to transform the education of students of color, it may become a necessary tool to NLERAP's durability.

I recommend this handbook to all educators who are trying to figure out how to transform classroom teaching and teacher preparation for communities of color. While the book's cultural, historic, and curricular specifics apply most directly to Latino/as, the intergenerational curriculum model and its infrastructure provide a roadmap that can inspire projects involving diverse communities working toward similar goals.

—Christine Sleeter

REFERENCES

Achinstein, B., & Ogawa, R. (2011). Change(d) agents: New teachers of color in urban schools. *Teachers College Record, 113*(11), 2503–2551.

Boyle-Baise, L., & Sleeter, C. E. (2000). Community-based service learning for multicultural teacher education. *Educational Foundations, 14*(2), 33–50.

Cabrera, N. L., Milem, J. F., Jaquette, O., & Marx, R. W. (2014). Missing the (student achievement) forest for all the (political) trees: Empiricism and the Mexican American student controversy in Tucson. *American Educational Research Journal, 51*(6), 1084–1118.

Flores, B. B., Clark, E. R., Claeys, L., & Villarreal, A. (2007). Academy for teacher excellence: Recruiting, preparing, and retaining Latino teachers though learning communities. *Teacher Education Quarterly, 34*(4), 53–69.

Franquiz, M. E., & Salazar, M. del C. (2004). The transformative potential of humanizing pedagogy: Addressing the diverse needs of Chicano/Mexicano students. *High School Journal, 87*(4), 36–54.

Moll, L. C., Gonzalez, N., Amanti, C., & Neff, D. (1992). Funds of knowledge for teaching: A qualitative approach to connect households and classrooms. *Theory into Practice, 31*(2), 132–141.

Ochoa, G. L. (2007). *Learning from Latino teachers*. San Francisco, CA: Jossey Bass.

Murrell, P. C., Jr. (2001). *The community teacher*. New York, NY: Teachers College Press.

Sleeter, C. E. (2008). Preparing white teachers for diverse students. In M. Cochran-Smith, S. Feiman-Nemser, J. McIntyre, & K. Demers (Eds.). *Handbook of research in teacher education: Enduring issues in changing contexts* (3rd ed.) (pp. 559–582), New York, NY: Routledge.

Sleeter, C. E., Neal, L. I., & Kumashiro, K. K. (Eds.). (2015). *Diversifying the teacher workforce*. New York, NY: Routledge.

NLERAP's Guiding Principles and Expected Teacher Competencies

On May 12 and August 8, 2010, the National Latino/a Education Research and Policy Project (NLERAP) Council met at the University of Texas at Austin and at Hunter College in New York, respectively, to establish, among other things, the following guiding principles of our organization that we agree honor the truth in our roots as an organization:

Promote social justice and democratic ideals.
Honor sociocultural perspectives.
Address the sociopolitical context of Latino/a communities.
Co-educate and co-create with communities.
Affirm an ethic of care, respect, trust, and mutuality in relationships.
Be inclusive.
Act with integrity.

Armed with the competencies that we as NLERAP members hope our approach will help cultivate in others, we aim to infuse the teaching ranks across all of our sites with teachers who are able to accomplish the following in their future classrooms:

- Affirm and build upon the linguistic and cultural heritage of Latino/a students.
- Develop critical literacies in the areas of reading, writing, numeracy, science, personal financial, and cultivate sociocultural and political awareness.
- Foster critical thinking skills among students that will facilitate their intellectual and social endeavors.
- Nurture a commitment to community participation, action, and civic engagement among students.
- Foster students' physical, spiritual, and emotional well-being.

Mini-Ethnography
Community, District, School, and Classroom Study

Editor's Note: This mini-ethnographic study derives from an educational foundations, social justice course (EDUC 364) taught by National Latino/a Education Research and Policy Project (NLERAP) colleagues in the context of California State University, Sacramento's Grow Your Own Teacher Education Institutes (GYO-TEI) initiative.

Project Overview

There are several purposes for this project, including: (1) helping you to develop an understanding of the macro- and microcultures of student teaching placements; (2) helping you to make professional and personal connections with your Sacramento State colleagues as you work as a team; (3) building an overall sense of the "funds of knowledge" that Sacramento-area students possess; and (4) preparing you for the Performance Assessment for California Teachers (PACT) exam, especially Task 1, but the observation, interpretation, and reflection skills will be helpful across all of the PACT tasks.

Project Timeline

First, you will collect data about the macro cultures of the community, district, and school site (Parts I and II) in teams (usually two to four student teachers assigned to the same school site). Then, you will explore the micro-setting of your classroom and complete the final analysis and reflection individually (Parts III and IV).

Adapted and modified by José Cintrón, PhD, from CSUS CoE San Juan PDS Center, Rio Linda Center, and Karen Benson, PhD, CSUS/CoE (Emerita).

Part I: Data collection due (early fall; allow 3 weeks for
   completion)
Part II: Data collection due (early November)
Part III: Data collection due (late November)
Part IV. Submit final product (synthesis of Parts I–III and Part IV)
   (early December)

You will enter your student teaching with an "outsider's view," or etic
perspective. Over the semester, however, you will develop more of
an "insider's view," or emic perspective, as you increasingly see your
classroom through the eyes of those who live and work in your school
placement and surrounding community/neighborhood. This assignment will allow you to collect data from a variety of perspectives and,
through analysis and reflection, to develop a robust understanding of
the students, families, and school site colleagues with whom you will
be working.

Basics of Ethnographic Inquiry into School Settings

- Observation is at the heart of any ethnographic investigation.
  It is a skill that requires one to open up and be perceptive. It
  also is imperative to understand and reflect upon one's own
  perceptions when encountering situations or experiences that
  are new, different, or even challenging.
- Remember that what you observe and perceive is always
  heavily influenced by your "lived experience" (guided by your
  personal values, worldview, culture, etc.). Multiple eyes and
  perspectives are essential when seeking to make accurate and
  useful interpretations based on observations.
- The kinds of resources available in a particular community
  may or may not be familiar to teachers. Some resources
  assumed by teachers to be accessible may not be available in
  all neighborhoods.
- Resources include private and public aspects of a community.
  They are both physical and cultural. For example, a large
  vacant lot might be a resource for environmental education.
  An ethnic food store, a community center, or church might be
  an appropriate site for a field trip that fits a particular unit of
  instruction.

- All communities have "funds of knowledge" (González, Moll & Amanti, 2005) that can enrich and contextualize instruction in order to enable teachers to understand their students' worlds.

PART I: THE COMMUNITY/NEIGHBORHOOD (GROUP) DATA COLLECTION (DUE [EARLY FALL; ALLOW 3 WEEKS FOR COMPLETION])

You will conduct the initial data collection for this mini-ethnography in student teams (usually two to four student teachers) assigned to the same school site. Your goal is to learn as much as you can about the school community/neighborhood and to gather and prepare the discussion in your course breakout sessions.

Suggestions for Observational Data Collection

- Create different roles within your group (photographers/ videographers, note takers, etc.) and work together to gather as much data as possible about the school's surroundings.
- Drive around in the neighborhood. Survey the general area first, and then go to more specific sites within it.
- Stop at places that look interesting; get out and explore. You should do a team "walking tour," taking photos/videos (if appropriate) and observational notes while doing this.
- Try to imagine what resources this neighborhood holds for a student. For example, where are the work opportunities, the parks, the hangouts? Explore specific areas in the neighborhood: gathering places for students and adults, community centers, coffee cafés, restaurants, sports areas, entertainment venues, gardens, public spaces that are particular to a specific cultural group (e.g., community garden), places of worship, markets, and so forth.
- What kind of services aid and support families (nonprofits, government agencies, libraries, and so on) in the neighborhood?
- Note the different religious organizations/affiliations or churches found in the community.

- What kinds of transportation services are available; is there a bus line?
- What kind of recreation (movie theaters, parks, pools) and/ or community centers are found within the community? Are these easily accessible to children and families? How many parks are there, and what are the conditions of the parks (e.g., are there picnic tables, benches, walking trails, swings, clean restrooms, etc.)?

You can collect additional data through interviews and web-based research (e.g., make use of sites such as http://www.neighborhoodscout .com).

Demographic Profile

- Using available demographic information (e.g., 2012 U.S. Census), what are the dominant cultural/ethnic groups in the neighborhood? What is the population of each? Where do they live in the neighborhood?
- Are there cultural areas in the neighborhood that represent these groups? Do any cultural groups host holiday gatherings or other celebrations in the neighborhood?
- Is there a central gathering place in the neighborhood? What group(s) congregates there?
- What is the annual income of families in the neighborhood?
- What types of employment are available for families?

Housing

- Do the majority of families own or rent?
- What is the mean price for a home?
- What is the average rent for apartments?
- How would you describe the homes, apartments, streets: well kept, in need of repairs, barricaded windows, fences, abandoned vehicles, and so forth? Focus on "social class" (i.e., high, middle, or low income). What supports your assumptions and conclusions?

Services

- What kind of services aid and support families (nonprofits, government agencies, libraries, etc.) in the neighborhood?
- Note the different religious organizations/affiliations or churches found in the community.
- What kinds of transportation services are available; is there a bus line?

Parks and Recreation

- What kind of recreation (movie theaters, parks, pools) and/ or community centers are within the community? Are these easily accessible to children and families, within walking distance, for instance?
- How many parks are there, and what are the conditions of the parks (e.g., are there picnic tables, benches, walking trails, swings, clean restrooms, etc.)?

General Geographic Setting

- Are there any features that are worth noting—for example, proximity to a highway or to railroad tracks? Do any of these features act as a barrier? Is the school connected to the surrounding community? Is the school viewed as an asset or liability?

PART II: THE DISTRICT AND SCHOOL (GROUP) DATA COLLECTION (DUE [PROVIDE EARLY NOVEMBER DATE])

The focus in this section is the district/school where you're student teaching.

1. **District History:**
   » Gather information on the following: city where district is located; when founded; what cities comprise the district; particular important events; people; occupations; crime;

recent structural/governance changes; superintendent;
district officials; and so forth.

» Evaluate the district website(s):
  – How informative and user-friendly is the site? Are
    the links accessible? Describe the aesthetics of the
    website (e.g., professional looking, appealing, busy,
    functional). Is it in English and/or are other languages
    employed?
  – What impression does the website give you of the
    district?
  – How would you rate/describe the website's information
    for prospective families, teachers, and community
    members, and its information on school board
    meetings, minutes, projects, accountability reports?

2. **Family Support Services/Programs:** Are there programs
   such as Healthy Start and English as a Second Language
   (ESL)? Do any programs offer a parent newsletter? If so,
   how often is it published? Do any programs offer a parent
   handbook? If so, what does it contain, how user-friendly is it,
   and does it also support families who speak other languages?

3. **District Demographics:** What is the age of neighborhood
   residents? Is it a district with declining enrollment, in which
   there are more older families than families with young
   children? What is the overall economic status? Gather
   data on numbers living in poverty, ethnic groups and their
   populations, and languages spoken.

4. **District-Wide Programs:** Gather information on programs
   for pregnant teens/parenting, foster youth, summer school
   (include texts used for subject areas and their publishers),
   intervention programs, enrichment programs, and so forth.

5. **Costs/Expenditures:**
   » Per-pupil spending
   » District rank statewide in spending
   » Salaries of district personnel, teachers, principals
   » Bond measures or parcel taxes
   » Other expenditures or revenues

6. **District Accountability:**
   » District rank statewide
   » How many schools have met adequate yearly
     progress (AYP) goals? Indicate the number of schools

undergoing Program Improvement or under sanctions—
provide particulars if available (e.g., performance
metrics).

School Profile

1. **School Information:** location; age of school; type of school
   (Title I, charter, etc.)
2. **School Demographics:** ethnic/cultural groups, languages,
   English language learner population, special education
   students, and so forth
   » School's attendance boundaries; any "feeder" schools
   » Enrollment: Does the school exceed recommended
     enrollment? Where are the "overflow" students sent? Is it
     an open-enrollment school? Is there a selection process?
     A lottery? Is it a magnet school? Are some students
     rejected? If so, why?
   » Transportation: How many students ride buses, use
     personal transportation, or walk to school? Do students
     live in the area surrounding the school?
   » Grade levels served; class size average by grade level
   » Poverty rate (determined by number of students on free/
     reduced lunch); mobility rate
   » Education level of parents
   » Qualifications of the teachers/staff (note how many
     teachers, if any, are on emergency permit); how many
     are No Child Left Behind (NCLB) qualified
   » Behavior statistics (suspensions, expulsions)
3. **School's Public Image/Culture:**
   » First impressions: Be as descriptive as possible. What
     does your first impression say to you about what
     all members of the community/school think of the
     school? Obtain a campus map, if available, to note
     areas of interest (e.g., garden plots, outdoor learning
     areas, etc.).
   » Maintenance: Are outdoor areas clean and well
     maintained? Are there gravel, paved, or grassy areas
     for play or aesthetics? Are the buildings clean and well
     maintained? Are there any problems with graffiti? What
     kind of security system is used? Are any windows barred,

broken, or boarded? Are paint and furniture clean and maintained (include the multipurpose center, library, restrooms)?

» Accessibility: Consider gates/fences, limited access (only one entrance), clear directions to visitors, adequate parking, and safety coming to and leaving school.

» Office and Support Areas/Staff: How is the office set up? Note the number of staff members and their positions (e.g., nurse, counselor, attendance clerk). Are the staff members inviting/welcoming? Are there bulletin boards with information/fliers posted for families about district and school events? Is children's work displayed in halls and classrooms? If so, what kind? Is there a parent organization(s) or site management team?

» Schoolwide management system: What discipline/ behavior management programs are used (e.g., schoolwide rules/consequences, Second Step, conflict resolution/mediators [students participation])? What support systems are used?

» Hallways and passageways: Are they clean and well lit? Is anything displayed in these areas (e.g., murals, pictures, artwork)?

» Are there video monitors? If so, what content do they display?

» Programs: Describe whether the site offers any of the following programs: bilingual (type—early, late, immersion), English language support, full inclusion, family literacy, parent English language programs, Linked Learning, Career Pathways, tutoring, after-school programs (homework, child care, sports).

» Other areas: Evaluate the library, resource room, staff lounge, nurse area, and other such locations. What do these look like? How are they equipped and staffed? Make note of full-time and part-time staff and the use of parent volunteers. Particularly evaluate the library—is it spacious? What equipment does it offer? Is a librarian and/or volunteer available (days/times)? What type of holdings and programs does it offer?

» Computer labs, technology, wireless access: Assess hardware and software resources.

» Other people's impressions: It is useful and informative if you are able to interview your cooperating teacher, a student, a staff person, and/or a parent (begin with a parent volunteer or a parent who participates in site management and/or PTO/PTA).

4. **Achievement Data**

» Using demographic data from the school, examine the achievement ranks of the subgroups in the school. How do they rank within the district and within the state?

» Note the school's most recent Academic Performance Index (API) and AYP rankings. Is the school under any sanctions? If so, what sanctions, and for how long?

» What are the factors influencing success/failure/struggle?

» What resources does the school provide for the families of the "underperforming" group(s)?

» How does the school support the learning of English language learner students and culturally different students, including students with special needs?

» How many students go on to college (percentage)?

PART III: THE CLASSROOM (COMPLETED INDIVIDUALLY) DATA COLLECTION (DUE [PROVIDE LATE NOVEMBER DATE])

The focus in this section is your individual student teaching classroom.

- *Classroom Demographics:* Who are the students? Consider gender, ethnicity, English language learners, special needs (this may not be obvious—such as students who go to resource rooms on an individualized education program [IEP]—you can ask the teacher about the needs of students in the classroom), and social class (free/reduced lunch, etc.).

- *Classroom Description:* Are rooms spacious, or are students packed into classrooms, with little room to move around or reconfigure seating arrangements? Are rooms well equipped, clean, colorful, well lit, and well ventilated? Is it too hot, too cold? What's displayed on the walls—is there student work displayed? If so, what kind, and how is it displayed?

- *Room Arrangement:* How does the teacher arrange students' work areas (desks/tables)—in rows, groups? (Of course, given the limited opportunities to be in the classroom, your observations cannot be used to make a judgment about the teacher's preferred style.)

- *Grouping*: Are students grouped (by achievement) for reading and math? Are there all levels in the classroom, or do students change classrooms for these subjects?
- *Classroom Management:* Describe rules, routines, procedures, and management strategies, and how students respond to these.
- *Teacher–Student Interactions:* How are students treated? Describe and characterize the teacher's response to students (e.g., how the teacher greets students at the beginning of the day; how the teacher talks with students during instruction, transitions, and noninstructional opportunities). Describe and characterize how students respond to the teacher, and to each other. For example, is humor employed (if yes, describe)?
- *Instructional Design*: What strategies does the teacher use? Describe student participation. How does the teacher call on students? Describe the type of questioning strategies the teacher uses—format (e.g., "verbal fill in the blanks," open-ended questions), clarification, extension. Does the teacher ask students to justify answers (e.g., "why" or "tell me more" questions)? How does the teacher check for understanding?

PART IV: ANALYSIS/REFLECTION (COMPLETED INDIVIDUALLY)

Final submission of all parts
(DUE [provide early December date])

In this final section you are asked to pause, reflect, synthesize, and interpret the data gathered by your team; this is a personal activity, not a group one. Here you are stepping back to take a panoramic view of all of the data you and your group collected and to make sense of the information for yourself.

What data are most helpful to you as you develop curriculum and instruction for your students? In what ways has completing a mini-ethnography of the setting in which you are student teaching supported the ideals of "rigor, relevance, and relationship" in your teaching? What questions about social justice in education emerged for you as you completed this assignment? Consider specific questions that you thought about in each of the previous categories (Parts I–III). Conclude with personal reflections about the impact of this study on you as a future educator.

Assignment Write-Up Instructions

Although data-collection tasks were divided among group members, each person will be responsible for writing up the information on their assigned section(s) and writing a personal conclusion/reflection on the overall mini-ethnography—specifically, what was learned and the implications for teaching now and in the future.

Format

- Title Page: Include names of team members, district, and school.
- Introduction: Discuss how the group decided on the data-collection process, what obstacles were encountered, how these were resolved, and so forth.
- Table of Contents: List sections with the name of the person responsible for data analysis and reporting for that section. In addition to the information on that section, each individual will include an introduction to his or her respective section.
- Analysis/Reflection: Include the reflections/analyses of each individual member.
- Reference Pages: Cite all sources employed—interviews, observations, websites, journals, photos, and so forth. Use consistent formatting (e.g., APA style).
- Format: The final submission should be approximately 15 to 20 pages (12-point font, double-spaced), assembled in a binder.

REFERENCE

González, N., Moll, L. C., & Amanti, C. (2005). (Eds.). *Funds of knowledge: Theorizing practices in households, communities, and classrooms.* NJ: Lawrence Erlbaum Associates.

WEBSITE RESOURCES

Ed-Data: www.ed-data.k12.ca.us/welcome.asp
District USD: www.district.edu
U.S. Census Bureau: www.factfinder.census.gov/home/saff/main.html?_lang=en

Transforming Deficit Myths About Language, Culture, and Literacy

Barbara Flores

Myth 1. "At-risk"/English language learner (ELL) children have a language problem. Their language and culture are deficient because they are poor and do not speak English.

Why True   Why Not True

Myth 2. "At-risk"/ELL children have problems because their parents don't care, can't read, or don't work with them.

Why True   Why Not True

Myth 3. These bilingual/ELLs have problems learning English because their Spanish/Mother Tongue interferes.

Why True   Why Not True

Slightly modified from Flores, B., Cousin, P., & Diaz, E. (1991). Transforming deficit myths about learning, language, and culture. *Language Arts*, *68*(5), 369–379.

Myth 4. Standardized tests can accurately identify and categorize
students who are "at risk" for learning and language "problems."
Why True   Why Not True

Myth 5. "At-risk"/ELL children need to be separated from the regular
mainstream classroom and taught according to their level on
required statewide English language proficiency tests.
Why True   Why Not True

Naming, Interrogating, and Transforming Deficit Myths, Fallacies, and "Habitudes"

Barbara Flores

1. Latino/a and Black students don't do well in school because they are poor.
2. Latino/a and Black students' parents don't care, don't help them at home, and can't read, so this is why "these" kids fail in school.
3. Spanish-speaking children need to abandon their first language, identity, and culture in order to "make it" in this society.
4. Learning English guarantees individuals that they will succeed in this society and in school.
5. A score on a standardized test measures a child's ability in an academic subject.
6. When a child code switches, this means that the child does not know either language well.
7. Scripted lessons help a teacher to teach students.
8. When a student can read so many words in a minute, this means that the student is a proficient reader.
9. Racism does not exist among and between Latino families, among and between Black families, or among and between races.
10. Teachers' beliefs, ideologies, and attitudes do not matter when teaching linguistically, culturally, ethnically, racially, and economically diverse students.

Slightly modified from Flores, B. (1982). *Language interference or influence: Toward a theory for Hispanic bilingualism* (Unpublished doctoral dissertation). University of Arizona, Tucson, AZ.

BaFa BaFa
Cross-Cultural Diversity/Inclusion Simulation Overview

BaFa BaFa is face-to-face learning simulation intended to improve students' cultural competency by helping them understand the impact of culture on the behavior of people and organizations. Students experience "culture shock" by visiting and trying to interact with a culture different from their own and in which people have different values and different ways of behaving, communicating, and solving problems.

Simulation Procedures

Two simulated cultures are created: an Alpha culture and a Beta culture. The director briefs the students on the general purposes of the simulation and then assigns them membership in either the Alpha or Beta culture. Each group moves into its own area, where members are taught the respective values, expectations, and customs of their new culture. Once all members understand and feel comfortable with their new culture, each culture sends an observer to the other. The observers attempt to learn as much as possible about the values, norms, and customs of the other culture without directly asking questions. After a few minutes, both observers return to their respective cultures and report on what they have observed.

Based on the report of the observer, each group develops hypotheses about the most effective way to interact with the other culture.

Created by Gary R. Shirts, Simulation Training Systems, San Diego, CA (see Shirts, 1993).

After the hypotheses have been formulated, the participants take turns visiting the other culture in small groups (three participants per visit). After each visit (approximately 2 minutes), the visitors report their observations to their groups. The groups use the data to test and improve their hypotheses for subsequent visitations. When everyone has had a chance to visit the other culture, the simulation ends.

The students then come together in one group to discuss, debrief, and analyze their experiences. Optimally, the simulation works well with 30 participants with 15 members in each culture and takes approximately 3.5 hours to complete.

Rationale/Purpose

By participating in this simulation students will come to experience the development and impact of stereotypes. By developing a deliberately narrow and stereotypical view of a "foreign culture," and subsequently examining their own reactions to this culture, and the other culture's stereotypical reaction to them, students come to understand the negative impact of stereotypes and the need to foster greater appreciation and recognition of others in all spheres of life.

Learning Objectives

1. To help students come to understand the meaning and impact of culture;
2. To demonstrate how one's feelings of attachment to a given culture are learned through the processes of socialization and that one's tendency to judge other cultures is based on one's own cultural perspective;
3. To demonstrate the potential for misinterpretation that arises when one evaluates another culture solely from the perspective of one's own values;
4. To build awareness of the extent to which cultures vary (cultural difference) and to help students work to understand, respect, and affirm these differences;
5. To help students appreciate, respect, and affirm cultural diversity, and to examine their attitudes and behaviors towards others who are "different" from themselves.

BaFa BaFa Reflection

The cultures represented in BaFa BaFa are designed to catch the essence of the differences between cultures without replicating a culture. Real cultures are infinitely more complex. It might be said that Beta language, for example, is to real language as the Beta or Alpha culture is to an existing culture.

Respond to the following reflection questions regarding your participation in the simulation:

1. Is it possible to talk about another culture without using evaluative terms? Explain your response.
2. If given a choice of membership, which culture would you choose and why?
3. In your opinion, what are the advantages of being "color blind"? What are the disadvantages? Describe the possible implications of your response for teaching and learning.
4. Describe your feelings during and after the debriefing. Explain why you were feeling in the manner you describe.

White Privilege
Unpacking the Invisible Knapsack Activity

Overview

What is White privilege? It is (1) a right, advantage, or immunity granted to or enjoyed by White persons beyond the common advantage of all others, and an exemption in many particular cases from certain burdens or liabilities; (2) a special advantage or benefit of White persons, with reference to divine dispensations, natural advantages, gifts of fortune, genetic endowments, social relations, and so forth.

Activity Procedures

Students and the instructor will read Peggy McIntosh's *White Privilege**
essay and then participate in the following activity. At the conclusion of the personal task, the instructor will have students form into groups (four or five students) to share their personal responses with one another. After the group component, the instructor will share his or her personal responses, and then ask for one student volunteer per group to share with the entire class. The instructor will be cognizant to select students representing different groups (male/female, students of color, older students, among other groups, if applicable) found in the class.

---

*See The National SEED Project (www.nationalseedprojet.org) for the essay *White Privilege and Male Privilege: A Personal Account of Coming to See Correspondences Through Work in Women's Studies (1988)*, written by Peggy McIntosh, the Founder and former Co-Director of the Wellesley Centers for Women, Wellesley, MA.

Created by José Cintrón, Ph.D., CSUS/CoE, Teaching Credentials Branch, Sacramento, CA.

PEGGY MCINTOSH WHITE PRIVILEGE ACTIVITY

As you begin this activity, it's important to make a distinction between *discretionary* and *nondiscretionary* privileges. These often are ambiguous in some of the contexts on McIntosh's White privileges list.

The rejection of a discretionary privilege is a personal responsibility and often a difficult and painful decision to make. That is, you have the "power" to reject said privilege. Nondiscretionary privileges function whether you want them to or not; in other words they are "beyond your control." With these you seldom have the "power" (i.e., political, economic, gender, and so forth) to reject them; hence you are obligated to take on a more proactive stance in order to effect a positive change towards a more just and equitable society.

Almost all privileges are *nondiscretionary,* highlighting the fact that the "system," rather than the individual, needs to change in order to mitigate or eliminate the privileges. The issue here is not to turn the analysis toward feelings of guilt for what ancestors, parents, or society may have done, but rather to acknowledge the effects of privilege—in other words, "open your eyes." Guilt is only appropriate for decisions one makes that are under one's own control. Most of these privileges are not under the privileged person's control, thus guilt is misplaced.

The goal is about transformation of oneself and ultimately of a broader community. After personal transformation comes strategizing what steps to take next to facilitate a clearer and more profound dialogue about coalition building across race, ethnicity, class, gender, sexual orientation, social economic status, and so forth. A sense of justice and equity is all that is required to provide motivation for dispelling and combating these privileges, not a sense of guilt. White privilege is socially constructed (as is race) and bestowed/inherited, not personally chosen.

With this as an introduction, the following activity has two components, a personal and a group component. Take your time and be thoughtful and honest with your responses. After completion of the personal element, the instructor will ask students to form groups of four to five to share responses.

Individual Task

1. Carefully read the McIntosh White Privileges Sheet.
2. Circle the privileges from the numbered list on the sheet that you think apply to you. Total: _____.

3. As best you can, situate the privileges into the following categories: race/ethnicity (R/E), social economic class (SEC), gender (G), skin color (SC), sexual orientation (SO), language (L), religion (R), age (A), size (S), geographic location (GL), professional status (PS), educational level (EL), or not applicable (NA). If there are other categories that you think better represent the privileges, indicate so.

4. Now categorize the personal privileges that are discretionary (i.e., privileges that you can opt to exercise or not exercise) and nondiscretionary (i.e., privileges that you possess whether you want them or not). Total: _____.

Group Task

1. Think of a time (or times) when you felt "advantaged/disadvantaged" due to race/ethnicity (R/E), social economic class (SEC), gender (G), skin color (SC), sexual orientation (SO), language (L), religion (R), age (A), size (S), geographic location (GL), professional status (PS), and/or educational level (EL). Share the most the most impactful experience with the group.

2. Share with the group which of your privileges are discretionary and which are non-discretionary.

3. Select your top two privileges. Explain to the group why you chose them.

4. Acknowledging my personal privileges made me feel _____. Share and explain your statement with the group.

Critical Pedagogy Framework for Creative Reflection

Phase I. Descriptive

The questions in this phase address how an individual describes/views his or her world and the issue to be addressed. This is the initial phase that allows us to describe what we hear and read, to define the issue or item. It's the what, when, where, by whom, and why questions. How does what has been said or written contribute to the understanding of the issues?

- Name the problem
- Put the problem in context = history/origin/causes
- Continue to problematize = identify elements
- Consequences

Phase II. Personal/Interpretive

This is the personal cognitive and affective interpretive phase. Here we dialogue about what we think and how we are feeling about the content of the information—for example, what does culture mean to human beings? How are these ideas related to my professional life/ activities? How do they relate to (contradict, complement, validate, enhance) my previous knowledge and/or experiences? What feelings or emotions do they provoke? What understanding (inspiration, strength, challenge) do they bring to my own personal quest or adventure as a human being?

- How does this information contradict, expand, differ from, or support personal previous experiences?

Adapted from Ada, A. F., & Beutel, C. M. (1993). *Participatory research as a dialogue for social action.* Unpublished manuscript, University of San Francisco, San Francisco, CA.

- What feelings and emotions are brought up by this reflection?
- How can we express our caring for others, and create a more nurturing situation?

Phase III. Critical/Multicultural

In this phase, we reflect on the information—we dialogue with information. Ask what benefits this will bring, who is involved, what the hidden agenda is, and so forth.

Do the premises presented here make sense to me? Why or why not? What would be the consequences of following these ideas? Whom do they benefit? How? What is acceptable, valuable? How do they relate to other positions? Are there any biases, or limitations, on these ideas? Would they be equally acceptable for all human beings? Why or why not? What other alternatives are there? What further questions do they suggest? What additional information do I now need?

- Ethical issues? Concerns?
- How does this situation support or deny or go against justice, equality, inclusion, and/or peace?
- Who benefits and who suffers from the conditions created?
- What structures support the conditions of the existing paradigm and/or stand in the way of effecting change?
- What is the paradigm?
- How would different people view this reality depending on their culture, ethnicity, socioeconomic conditions, gender, age, sexual orientation, and /or religion?

Phase IV. Creative/Transformative
(Action that leads toward transformation)

During this phase we move to changing the world—it is an action question. For example, how can culture be validated and transmitted in a liberating way? What can I integrate into my teaching/professional practice based on these presentations, writings, and reflections? How do these ideas help to empower me to struggle for the transformation of reality from the "what is" to the "what ought to be"?

- What actions can I/we generate based on the previous reflections to bring about a more just reality?

Group Work and Second Language Learner Planner

Unit/Lesson _____

Targeted Content and ELD Standards _____

What skill-building activities will you frontload to reinforce group-work norms, roles, and expectations?	
How will you group your students so that they serve as academic and language resources for each other?	
How does the group-work task require positive interdependence?	

What language supports (written and verbal) will you provide for your English learners?	
Define clear outcomes for the group-work (content, language, social, and so forth).	
How and what will you assess at the individual student level? Align assessment(s) with targeted standards and outcomes.	
How and what will you assess at the group level? Align assessment(s) with targeted standards and outcomes.	

Productive Group Work Rubric

Appendix I. Productive Group Work Rubric

INDICATORS	4—Exemplary	3—Applying	2—Approaching	1—Limited
Complexity of task: *The task is a novel application of the grade-level-appropriate concept and is designed so that the outcome is not guaranteed (a chance for productive failure exists).*	Task reflects purpose and what was modeled. Task allows students an opportunity to use a variety of resources to creatively apply their knowledge of what was modeled. Students have an opportunity to experiment with concepts.	Task provides multiple, clear opportunities for students to apply and extend what was modeled. Students have an opportunity to use a variety of resources to creatively apply their knowledge of what was modeled.	Task is somewhat reflective of the purpose of the lesson, but there is little opportunity for student experimentation or innovation.	Task is an exact replication of what was modeled, with little or no opportunity for student experimentation with concepts.
Joint attention to tasks or materials: *Students are interacting with one another to build on one another's knowledge. Outward indicators include body language and movements associated with meaningful conversations, and shared visual gaze on materials.*	Students ask critical questions of one another, developing and forming personal opinions and conclusions. They are able to evaluate and synthesize information, as well as independently use a variety of resources, to acquire new or unknown information.	Body language, visual gaze, and language interactions provide evidence of joint attention to the task or materials by all members of the group. Students can explain their contributions and the contributions of the other group members.	Body language, visual gaze, and language interactions provide some evidence of mutual attention to the task or materials by most members. Students are not holding each other accountable for purposeful contributions.	Students divide up the tasks so that they can do their work, then meet near the end to assemble components. Body language, visual gaze, and lack of language interactions provide evidence of independent work occurring within the group.

(Continued)

Appendix I. Productive Group Work Rubric (Continued)

Argumentation not arguing: *Students use accountable talk to persuade, provide evidence, ask questions of one another, and disagree without being disagreeable.*	Students reach a better understanding or consensus based on evidence and opinions provided by others. Students hold each member of the group accountable by using questioning strategies and evidence to persuade or disagree. The conversation is respectful and courteous.	Students ask for and offer evidence to support claims. However, members continue to maintain initial beliefs or positions about topics without considering arguments of others. The conversation is generally respectful, but some members may not participate.	There's a process in place for accountable talk. However, student dialogue is limited, and there are minimal efforts to support the product. Conversation is generally respectful, but is often dominated by one member of the group or veers off topic.	No clear processes in place to facilitate accountable talk. Lack of structure is evident, as students are off task, in conflict, and/or unable to complete product.
Language support: *Written, verbal, teacher, and peer supports are available to boost academic language usage.*	Sentence frames are differentiated based on students' proficiency and need. A wide range of frames is available for students, and students use the frames independently in academic language and writing. Teacher modeling includes the use of frames as well as academic vocabulary and high expectations for language production.	Students use one or two sentence frames from the variety that are available in a structured setting. A set of target vocabulary is available and used. Teachers model the use of frames. Students are encouraged to use language support and guided instruction to facilitate productive group work.	Academic language related to the concept/ standard is present. A frame is provided. The teacher models at least once using target vocabulary or language frame. Students are encouraged to attempt using target vocabulary without opportunities for guided practice.	Vocabulary is posted but its use is not modeled. Students are simply told to use the words. Language frames are not provided.

INDICATORS	4—Exemplary	3—Applying	2—Approaching	1—Limited
Teacher role: *What is the teacher doing while productive group work is occurring?*	Teacher is purposeful in scaffolding using prompts, cues, and questions, and checks for understanding regularly. Evidence collected during this time is use to plan for their instruction.	Some scaffolding and checking for understanding occurs but there are delays in corrections or changes to the instruction. There is a link to further instruction.	Scaffolding or checking for understanding occurs but is not used to plan further instruction.	Teacher manages, but does not interact with groups to scaffold conceptual knowledge.
Grouping: *Small groups of two to five students are purposefully constructed to maximize individual strengths without magnifying areas of needs (heterogenous grouping).*	Groups are flexible and change based on students' proficiency, academic need, and/or content area. Productive group work occurs throughout the day.	Purposeful heterogeneous grouping occurs, which is fluid in response to students' proficiency.	Some heterogeneous grouping occurs, but homogenous grouping practices dominate. Decisions based on assessment are not apparent.	Grouping practices are solely homogenous and are done primarily for scheduling convenience.

Source: Fisher & Frey, 2009.

Planning for Language and Content Integration

Content Objectives: Students Will Be Able To (SWBAT)	Language Functions Used to Carry Out Tasks:

Texts: Comprehension of Oral and Written Language	Tasks: Production, Interaction, Writing, Assessment

Discourse Demands: *Thinking Skills/ Message Organization*	Syntax Demands: *Sentence Structure, Grammar*	Lexical Demands: *Vocabulary, Figurative Language*

Language Objectives: SWBAT

Adapted from Ranney, Schornack, Maguire, and Dillard-Paltrineri (2014).

PAR Process Handout

The following handout presents a summarization with several key phases highlighted for implementing a participatory action research (PAR) project. The phases are not meant to be prescriptive steps, but rather suggested departure points for moving through a PAR process. Although the phases are presented in a linear fashion, a circular approach is most often used (i.e., phases are revisited and inform one another throughout the process). For example, although actions are listed in the final phase, these can actually take place much earlier in the process, or be the basis of the inquiry process itself. Integrated within the handout are activities for self- and collective inquiry drawn from the principles and activities in Chapter 4, "*PAR Entremundos:* A Practitioner's Guide," that the reader of this appendix should cross-reference throughout.

Phase 1—Construct PAR Collective

Participants in the PAR project are drawn from stakeholders at the site or community in which the inquiry/action will take place.

A community or collective may have been organized already prior to the implementation of a PAR project, such as with students in a particular classroom or school.

PAR Guide Resources

1. Principle of Participation—Example 1: Graduation Standards; Example 2: Social Justice Education Project (SJEP)
2. Principle of Critical Inquiry—Activity: Educational Dialogues

Phase 2—Identify Generative Themes

Generative themes are words that have social, political, or cultural meaning for PAR participants.

Poetry, music, or some other creative means may be used to identify generative themes. The themes typically evolve out of the experiences of the PAR participants and are rooted deeply in communities.

PAR Guide Resource

1. Principle of Participation—Activity 2: I Am Poetry

I Am Poem Template

I am (two special characteristics)
I wonder (something you are actually curious about)
I hear (an imaginary sound)
I see (an imaginary sight)
I want (an actual desire)
I am (the first line of the poem restated)
I pretend (something you actually pretend to do)
I feel (a feeling about something imaginary)
I touch (an imaginary touch)
I worry (something that really bothers you)
I cry (something that makes you very sad)
I am (the first line of the poem repeated)
I understand (something you know is true)
I say (something you believe in)
I dream (something you actually dream about)
I try (something you really make an effort about)
I hope (something you actually hope for)
I am (the first line of the poem repeated)

Phase 3—Problematize Generative Themes

- Generative themes are placed in problem form.
- Themes in problem form are discussed and analyzed to identify root causes of problems.
- PAR participants select project topics that address root causes.

PAR Guide Resources

1. Principle of Knowledge Co-construction—Activity 1: Dialogical Pedagogy; Activity 2: Problem Tree

Phase 4—Generate Research Protocol

- PAR participants develop research questions from topics addressing root causes.
- Methods for answering questions are placed in research protocol.

PAR Guide Resources

1. Principle of Critical Inquiry—Activity: Educational Dialogues
2. Principle of Creative Praxes—Activity 1: Maps; Activity 2: PhotoVoice
3. Research Process

Phase 5—Collect Data

- PAR participants collect data through methods listed in research protocol.
- PAR participants can use creative methods for collecting data (art, poetry, theater, photos, video, etc.).

PAR Guide Resources

1. Principle of Power With(in)—Example 2: Emotions Workshop; Activity 3: State Shifting
2. Research Process

Phase 6—Analyze Data

- PAR participants review data to locate information that answers research questions.
- Data are highlighted that answer questions and indicate relevant patterns.
- Highlighted data are grouped into codes or conceptual categories.

PAR Guide Resources

1. Principle of Power With(in)—Activity 4: Graffiti Walls
2. Principle of Indigenous Cosmologies—Activity 3: Movement Meditation
3. Research Process

Phase 7—Develop Findings and Create Offerings

- PAR participants identify relevant literature to support research topics.
- PAR participants take codes or conceptual categories and present them along with supporting data and relevant literature through traditional presentations (written papers, PowerPoint presentations) or creative means (art, poetry, dance, theater, photos, videos).

PAR Guide Resources

1. Principle of Indigenous Cosmologies—Activity 2: Theatre of the Oppressed
2. Principle of Creative Praxes—Example 2: Community Performance Theater
3. Principle of Transformational Action—Activity 1: Demonstrating Our Expertise: Reflections on Past Experience; Activity 2: Demonstrating Expertise: Presenting Research to a School District Board

Phase 8—Take Action and Dialogue with Community

- PAR participants present PAR projects to community members and key stakeholders and engage them in dialogue about their research topics.
- PAR participants present an action plan to key stakeholders to initiate change.

PAR Guide Resources

1. Principle of Transformational Action
2. Principle of *Concientización para la Colectiva*/Conscientization for the Collective

Frequently Asked Questions About PAR

Is PAR a method?

No, participatory action research (PAR) is not just a method. It is both an epistemology (a way of knowing) and an ontology (a way of being). It is an approach to doing research that assumes that people who are impacted by the topic or issue (e.g., students, community members, teachers, etc.) should be co-researchers. PAR can actually use many different methods, such as interviews, participant observation, surveys, mapping, and so forth. It can also use quantitative methods.

Isn't PAR biased?

Some argue that PAR is biased (or a form of advocacy) because community members, who have a stake in the outcome, are part of the process and can therefore make it less "objective." We feel that inclusion of community members in the research process can actually strengthen the validity of a study by drawing on the grounded knowledge, experiences, questions, and language of the community so that more relevant issues, questions, and framings are used.

Is PAR rigorous enough/is it "real" research?

Studies using PAR vary in rigor, just as any other research study or approach would. It is "real" research because the process of systematically investigating an issue should be followed. As with other types of research, there is good work and, well, not-so-good work. It is more of a matter of how it is carried out. We would also argue that PAR can be more rigorous than non-PAR approaches because of the potential relevance and authenticity.

How is PAR different from using qualitative strategies such as member checks, research informants, or triangulation?

Member checks and validity checks typically happen after a researcher collects data. For example, after conceptualizing the issue and carrying out the research, a person then checks with the community under study to see whether the themes ring true or should be revised. With the PAR approach, the "members" are part of the research team and part of the decision making throughout the entire process (not just at the end). Community members are not just "informants," but are partners in the research process. Triangulation is talking about using different methods and comparing them—it can be used within the PAR process but is not the same thing as PAR.

How is PAR different from action research?

PAR can claim different family trees. One is as an offshoot of action research, part of the Lewinian tradition that calls for research (typically in education settings) to go beyond simply understanding a particular issue to actually doing something about it. PAR has this in common with action research, but adds the idea of participation: It matters who is framing the issue, doing the research, and deciding what needs to be done about it. And *PAR Entremundos* specifically connects to the southern tradition, critical race and feminist theories, and indigenous cosmologies (see discussion of guiding principles in Chapter 4).

Isn't PAR just another ivory-tower academic approach disconnected from community?

PAR also has a family tree growing from social movements in Latin America as *investigación participativa* (not limited to education) in what some call the southern tradition. Some argue that this root starts with the community (not the academy), where people use research to name the oppressions they face toward conscientization and act against social injustices. It can be (and has been) connected to activist research and community organizing. There are many community-based organizations (CBOs) that practice PAR without any direct university connection. Community is an integral part of PAR; it is an approach premised on the participation of community members as partners in a collective research and action endeavor.

What is YPAR?

YPAR is participatory action research specifically with youth, usually in school or after-school settings.

How is PAR different from student-centered, inquiry/project-based learning pedagogies?

Classroom-based YPAR has a lot in common with these approaches to teaching and learning. With school-based PAR, typically, youth development is an additional goal, in terms of research and analytical skills, in addition to community engagement and activist/political participation. As such, its practice in a classroom setting has elements in common with both of these pedagogical approaches. The research aspect certainly involves an inquiry process. Engaging PAR can be considered in line with project-based learning, because you are completing a PAR project. The participatory nature of this work means that YPAR is a student-centered approach. Although the pedagogy of PAR can include all of these descriptions, just one of these cannot capture the entirety of the process and approach. These are perhaps best thought of as ingredients in the PAR meal/banquet. In PAR there are more explicit ideological commitments related to research, social justice, and action. For example, in PAR, the youth work with the teacher to decide on the research problem or project, rather than the teacher dictating the "what" and "how." And they are involved in the entire inquiry process, including the dissemination of the findings in their collective learning.

Isn't this just service learning?

Service learning is valuable in its own right. However, PAR has a somewhat different framing. Service can suggest that one group (with more power or privilege) is helping another (with less). PAR assumes more of a partnership between people working together toward a common project. PAR is more in the spirit of this quote by an Australian Aboriginal group: "If you have come to help me, you are wasting your time. But if your liberation is bound up in mine, then let us begin." Not all service learning is done this way; we are merely speaking of traditional framings of service and service learning. Some PAR projects actually may be conducted under the guise of service/service learning, thereby changing how service, a requirement in many schools, can be viewed. Sometimes, this question is meant to challenge the rigor of PAR. The research part of PAR must also be emphasized; service learning does not typically require that research (collecting and analyzing data, etc.) be conducted.

Reflective and cognizant that the conscious elimination of a "step-by-step" process might leave one with the question of "How can this be done?" and/or "What would this concretely look like in the classroom?" The case example provided in Chapter 5 models the integration of the principles, along with the research process and its foundation, according to the *PAR Entremundos* lens that we provide.

References

Achinstein, B., & Ogawa, R. (2011). Change(d) agents: New teachers of color in urban schools. *Teachers College Record, 113*(11), 2503–2551.

Achinstein, B., Ogawa, R. T., Sexton, D., & Freitas, C. (2010). Retaining teachers of color: A pressing problem and a potential strategy for "hard-to-staff schools." *Review of Educational Research, 80*(1), 71–107.

Ada, A. F. (2002). *A magical encounter: Latino children's literature in the classroom* (2nd ed.). Boston, MA: Pearson Education.

Ada, A. F., & Beutel, C. M. (1993). *Participatory research as a dialogue for social action*. Unpublished manuscript, University of San Francisco, San Francisco, CA.

Ahram, R., Stembridge, A., Fergus, E., & Noguera, P. (2011). *Framing urban school challenges: The problems to examine when implementing response to intervention*. Retrieved from Response to Intervention Network website: http://www.rtinetwork.org/learn/diversity/urban-school-challenges

Alva, S. (1991). Academic invulnerability among Mexican American students: The importance of protective resources and appraisals. *Hispanic Journal of Behavioral Sciences, 13*(1), 18–34.

Antrop-González, R., & De Jesús, A. (2006). Toward a theory of critical care in urban small school reform: Examining structures and pedagogies of caring in two Latino community based schools. *International Journal of Qualitative Studies in Education, 194*, 409–433.

Antrop-González, R., & Valenzuela, A. (2012). Caring theory in education. In J. Banks (Ed.), *Encyclopedia of diversity in education* (pp. 301–303). Thousand Oaks, CA: Sage.

Antrop-González, R., Vélez, W., & Garrett, T. (2003). *Where are the academically successful Puerto Rican students? Five success factors of high achieving Puerto Rican high school students* (Julian Samora Research Institute Working Paper No. 61). East Lansing, MI: Julian Samora Research Institute.

Antrop-González, R., Vélez, W., & Garrett, T. (2005). ¿Donde estan los estudiantes puertorriquenos academicamente exitoso? (Where are the academically successful Puerto Rican students?). Success factors of high achieving Puerto Rican high school students. *Journal of Latinos in Education, 2*, 74–95.

Anzaldúa, G. (1987). *Borderlands/La frontera:* The new *mestiza*. San Francisco, CA: Aunt Lute.

Anzaldua, G. (1997). La conciencia de la mestiza: Towards a new consciousness. In Garcia, A. M. (Ed.), *Chicana feminist thought: The basic historical writings* (pp. 270–274). New York, NY: Routledge.

Apple, M. (1996). *Cultural politics and education*. New York, NY: Teachers College Press.

Arrien, A. (1993). *The four-fold way: Walking the paths of the warrior, teacher, healer and visionary*. New York, NY: HarperOne.

Austin, J., & Hickey, A. (2008). Critical pedagogical practice through cultural studies. *International Journal of the Humanities, 6*(1), 133–139.

Ayala, J., Cammarota, J., Rivera, M., Torre, M., Rodriguez, L., & Berta-Avila, M. (forthcoming). *PAR Entremundos: A pedagogy of the Américas*.

Ball, D. L. (2010, May 4). *Summary of testimony to the U.S. House of Representatives Committee on Education and Labor*. Retrieved from Education and the Workforce Committee website: http://edworkforce.house .gov/uploadedfiles/5.4.10_ball.pdf

Barndt, D. (1998). The world in a tomato: Revisiting the use of "codes" in Freire's problem-posing education. *Convergence, 31*(1/2), 62–74.

Bartlett, L., & Garcia, O. (2011). *Additive schooling in subtractive times: Bilingual education and Dominican immigrant youth in the Heights*. Nashville, TN: Vanderbilt University Press.

Bartolomé, L. I. (2006). The struggle for language rights: Naming and interrogating the colonial legacy of "English only." *Human Architecture: Journal of the Sociology of Self-Knowledge, 4*(3), 25–32.

Bartolomé, L. I. (2008). *Ideologies in education: Unmasking the trap of teacher neutrality*. New York, NY: Peter Lang Publishing.

Bartolomé, L. I., & Balderrama, M. V. (2001). The need for educators with political and ideological clarity: Providing our children with "the best." In M. Reyes & J. J. Halcón (Eds.), *The best for our children: Critical perspectives on literacy for Latino students* (pp. 48–64). New York, NY: Teachers College Press.

Becker, E. (1967). *Beyond alienation: A philosophy of education for the crisis of democracy.* New York, NY: George Braziller, Inc.

Berliner, D. C. (2009, March). *Poverty and potential: Out-of-school factors and school success.* Boulder, CO: Education in the Public Interest.

Berta-Avila, M., Tijerina-Revilla, A., & Figueroa, J. (Eds.). (2011). *Marching students: Chicana and Chicano activism in education, 1968 to the present.* Reno, NV: University of Nevada Press.

Boal, A. (1993). *Theatre of the oppressed.* New York, NY: Theatre Communications Group.

Bourdieu, P. (1977). Cultural reproduction and social reproduction. In J. Karabel & A. H. Halsey (Eds.), *Power and ideology in education* (pp. 137–153). New York, NY: Oxford University Press.

Boyd, D., Grossman, P., Lankford, H., Loeb, S., & Wyckoff, J. (2005, December). *How changes in entry requirements alter the teacher workforce and affect student achievement* (NBER Working Paper No. 11844). Retrieved from National Bureau of Economic Research website: http://www.nber.org/papers/w11844

Brittain, C. (2009, April/May). Transnational messages: What teachers can learn from understanding students' lives in transnational social spaces. *High School Journal, 92*(4), 100–113.

Bronfenbrenner, U. (1979). *The ecology of human development.* Cambridge, MA: Harvard University Press.

Brown, S. (2010). *Play: How it shapes the brain, opens the imagination, and invigorates the soul.* New York, NY: Avery Trade.

Bruner, J. (1996). *The culture of education.* Cambridge, MA: Harvard University Press.

Bryson, B. (1996). "Anything but heavy metal": Symbolic exclusion and musical dislikes. *American Sociological Review, 61*(5), 884–899.

Caine, G., & Nummela-Caine, R. (1997). *Education on the edge of possibility.* Alexandria, VA: Association for Supervision and Curriculum Development.

Caine, G., Nummela-Caine, R., & Crowell, S. (1999). *Mindshifts: A brain-based process for restructuring schools and renewing education* (2nd ed.). Tucson, AZ: Zephyr Press.

Calderón, M., Slavin, R., & Sánchez, M. (2011). Effective instruction for English learners. *The Future of Children, 21*(1), 103–127.

Cambium Learning. (2004). *Curriculum audit: Mexican American Studies Department—Tucson Unified School District.* Retrieved from American Civil Liberties Union of Arizona website: http://www.acluaz .org/sites/default/files/documents/Ethnic%20studies%20audit%20 summary.pdf

Cammarota, J. (2004). The gendered and racialized pathways of Latina and Latino youth: Different struggles, different resistances. *Anthropology and Education Quarterly, 35*(1), 53–74.

Cammarota, J., & Fine, M. (Eds.). (2008). *Revolutionizing education: Youth participatory action research in motion.* New York, NY: Routledge.

Carr, P. R., & Klassen, T. R. (1997). Different perceptions of race in education: Racial minority and White teachers. *Canadian Journal of Education, 22,* 67–81.

Carter, T. P. (1970). *Mexican Americans in school: A history of educational neglect.* Princeton, NJ: College Entrance Examination Board.

Carter, T. P., & Segura, R. D. (1979). *Mexican Americans in school: A decade of change.* New York, NY: College Entrance Examination Board.

Center for Research on Education, Diversity & Excellence (CREDE). (2001). *Sociocultural factors in social relationships: Examining Latino teachers' and paraeducators' interactions with Latino students* (Research Report 9). Washington, DC: Author.

Cintli Rodriguez, R. (2014). *Our sacred maíz is our mother: Indigeneity and belonging in the Americas.* Tucson, AZ: University of Arizona Press.

Clark, E. R., & Flores, B. B. (2001). Who am I? The social construction of ethnic identity and self-perceptions in Latino preservice teachers. *The Urban Review, 33*(2), 69–86.

Clewell, B. C., Puma, M., & McKay, S. A. (2001). *Does it matter if my teacher looks like me? The impact of teacher race and ethnicity on student academic achievement.* New York, NY: Ford Foundation.

Colín, E. (2014). *Indigenous education through dance and ceremony: A Mexica palimpsest.* New York, NY: Palgrave Macmillan.

Collins, P. H. (1991). *Black feminist thought: Knowledge, consciousness, and the politics of empowerment.* New York, NY: Routledge.

Combahee River Collective. (1982). *A Black feminist statement.* In G. T Hull, P. B. Scott, & B. Smith (Eds.), *But some of us are brave: Black women's studies* (pp. 13–32). Old Westbury, NY: The Feminist Press.

Comer, J. P. (2006). *Child and adolescent development research and teacher education: Evidence-based pedagogy, policy, and practice*. Retrieved from National Council for Accreditation of Teacher Education (NCATE) website: http://www.ncate.org/dotnetnuke/LinkClick.aspx?fileticket =IKL54rTMZp8%3D&tabid=35

Cotera, M. (1976). *Diosa y hembra: The history and heritage of Chicanas in the US*. Austin, TX: Information Systems Development.

Dai, C., Sindelar, P. T., Denslow, D., Dewey, J., & Rosenberg, M. S. (2005). Economic analysis and the design of alternative-route teacher education programs. *Journal of Teacher Education, 58*(5), 422–439.

Dall'Alba, G., & Sandberg, J. (2006). Unveiling professional development: A critical review of stage models. *Review of Educational Research, 76*(3), 383–412.

Damasio, A. (1999). *The feeling of what happens: Body and emotion in the making of consciousness*. New York, NY: Harcourt.

Darder, A. (1997). Creating the conditions for cultural democracy in the classroom. In A. Darder, R. D. Torres, & H. Gutierrez (Eds.), *Latinos and education: A critical reader* (pp. 331–350). New York, NY: Routledge.

Darling-Hammond, L. (2000). Teacher quality and student achievement: A review of state policy evidence. *Education Policy Analysis Archives, 8*(1), 1–44. Retrieved from http://epaa.asu.edu/epaa/v8n1/

Darling-Hammond, L. (2003, May). Keeping good teachers: Why it matters, what leaders can do. *Educational Leadership, 60*(8), 6–13.

Darling-Hammond, L., & Bransford, J. (Eds.). (2005). *Preparing teachers for a changing world: What teachers should learn and be able to do*. Washington, DC: The National Academy of Education.

Day, J. (2007). *Being what you want to see: Bringing emotional mastery into everyday life*. San Bruno, CA: Shinnyo-en Foundation.

Daza, S. L., & Huckaby, M. F. (2014). *Terra incognita*: Em-bodied data analysis. *Qualitative Inquiry, 20*(6), 801–810.

De Jesús, A. (2007). El Puente Academy for Peace and Justice. In L. Díaz Soto (Ed.), *The Praeger handbook of Latino education in the U.S.* (Vol. 2, pp. 141–142). Westport, CT: Praeger.

Dee, T. S. (2004). Teachers, race, and student achievement in a randomized experiment. *Review of Economics and Statistics, 86*(1), 195–210.

Delgado, R., & Stefancic, J. (Eds.). (1999). *Critical race theory: The cutting edge.* Philadelphia, PA: Temple University Press.

Delgado-Bernal, D. (2001). Learning and living pedagogies of the home: The *mestiza* consciousness of Chicana students. *International Journal of Qualitative Students in Education, 14*(5), 623–639.

Delpit, L., & Dowdy, J. K. (Eds.). (2002). *The skin that we speak: Thoughts on language and culture in the classroom.* New York, NY: The New Press.

Dillard, C., Abdur-Rashid, D., & Tyson, C. A. (2006). My soul is a witness: Affirming pedagogies of the spirit. *Qualitative Studies in Education, 13*(5), 447–462.

Dillard, C. B. (2000). The substance of things hoped for, the evidence of things not seen: Examining an endarkened feminist epistemology in educational research and leadership. *International Journal of Qualitative Studies in Education, 13*(6), 661–681.

Dixon, E. J. (2000). *Bones, boats, and bison: Archeology and the first colonization of western North America.* Albuquerque, NM: New Mexico Press.

Duncan, A. (2010, November). *The new normal: Doing more with less—Secretary Arnie Duncan's remarks at the American Enterprise Institute.* Retrieved from U.S. Department of Education website: http://www.ed.gov/news/speeches/new-normal-doing-more-less-secretary-arne-duncans-remarks-american-enterprise-institut

Echevarría, J., Vogt, M., & Short, D. (2004). *Making content comprehensible for English learners.* Boston, MA: Allyn & Bacon.

Echevarría, J., Vogt, M., & Short, D. J. (2010). *Making content comprehensible for secondary English learners: The SIOP model.* Boston, MA: Pearson Education.

Egalite, A. J., Kisida, B., & Winters, M. A. (2015). Representation in the classroom: The effect of own-race teachers on student achievement. *Economics of Education Review, 45*, 44–52.

El Nasser, H. (2014, June 2). Latino millennials become a political force to reckon with. *Al Jazeera.* Retrieved from http://america.aljazeera.com/features/2014/6/latino-millennialselection2014.html

Espinoza-Herold, M. (2003). *Issues in Latino education: Race, school culture, and the politics of academic success.* Boston, MA: Allyn & Bacon.

Facio, E., & Lara, I. (Eds.). (2014). *Fleshing the spirit: Spirituality and activism in Chicana, Latina, and Indigenous women's lives.* Tucson, AZ: University of Arizona Press.

Fals-Borda, O., & Rahman, M. A. (1991). *Action and knowledge: Breaking the monopoly with participatory action research*. New York, NY: Apex Press.

Faltis, C., Arias, M. B., & Ramírez-Marín, F. (2010). Identifying relevant competencies for secondary teachers of English learners. *Bilingual Research Journal, 33*, 307–328.

Feagin, J. R., & Feagin, C. B. (2011). *Racial and ethnic relations* (9th ed.). Boston, MA: Pearson Education.

Fine, M. (2005). *Beyond silenced voices: Class, race, and gender in United States schools*. Albany, NY: State University of New York Press.

Fisher, D., & Frey, N. (2009). Productive group work rubric. Retrieved from http://www.scribd.com/doc/84723099/Productive-Group-Work-Rubric#scribd

Flores, B. (1982). *Language interference or influence: Toward a theory for Hispanic bilingualism* (Unpublished doctoral dissertation). University of Arizona, Tucson, AZ.

Flores, B. (2005). The intellectual presence of the deficit view of Spanish-speaking children in the educational literature during the 20th century. In P. Pedraza & M. M. Rivera (Eds.), *Latino education: An agenda for community action research* (pp. 75–99). Mahwah, NJ: Erlbaum.

Flores, B., Vasquez, O. A., & Clark, E. R. (2014). *Generating transworld pedagogy: Reimagining La Clase Mágica*. Lanham, MD: Lexington Books.

Flores-González, N. (1999, September). Puerto Rican high achievers: An example of ethnic and academic identity compatibility. *Anthropology & Education Quarterly, 30*(3), 343–362.

Foley, D. E., & Valenzuela, A. (2005). Critical ethnography: The politics of collaboration. In N. K. Denzin & Y. Lincoln (Eds.), *The handbook of qualitative research* (3rd ed., pp. 217–234). Beverly Hills, CA: Sage.

Four Arrows (Jacobs, D. T.), England-Aytes, K., Cajete, G., Fisher, M. R., Mann, B. A., McGaa, E., & Sorensen, M. (2013). *Teaching truly: A curriculum to indigenize mainstream education*. New York, NY: Peter Lang Publishing.

Freire, P. (1970). *Pedagogy of the oppressed*. New York, NY: Seabury Press.

Freire, P. (1993). *Pedagogy of the oppressed*. New York, NY: Continuum.

Freire, P. (1994). *Education for critical consciousness*. New York, New York: Continuum.

Freire, P. (1998). *The Paulo Freire reader* (M. A. Freire & D. Macedo, Eds.). New York, NY: Continuum Press.

Fry, R. (2008). *Latinos account for half of U.S. population growth since 2000*. Retrieved from Pew Hispanic Research Center website: http://www .pewhispanic.org/2008/10/22/latinos-account-for-half-of-us-population-growth-since-2000/

Fry, R., & Gonzáles, F. (2008). *One-in-five and growing fast: A profile of Hispanic public school students*. Retrieved from Pew Hispanic Research Center website: http://www.pewhispanic.org/2008/08/26/one-in-five-and-growing-fast-a-profile-of-hispanic-public-school-students/

Fry, R., & López, M. H. (August 20, 2012). *Hispanic student enrollments reach new highs in 2011: Now largest minority group on four-year college campuses*. Retrieved from Pew Hispanic Research Center website: http://www .pewhispanic.org/2012/08/20/hispanic-student-enrollments-reach-new-highs-in-2011/

Galeano, E. (1997). *Open veins of Latin America: Five centuries of the pillage of a continent*. New York, NY: Monthly Review Press.

Galindo, R. (1996). Reframing the past in the present: Chicana teacher role identity as a bridging identity. *Education and Urban Society, 29*(1), 85–102.

Galván, R. T. (2010). Calming the spirit and insuring supervivencia: Rural Mexican women-centered teaching and learning spaces. *Ethnography and Education, 5*(3), 309–323.

Galván, R. T. (2011). Chicana transborder vivencias and autoherteorías: Reflections from the field. *Qualitative Inquiry, 17*(6), 552–557.

Gándara, P., & Contreras, F. (2009). *The Latino education crisis: The consequences of failed social policies*. Cambridge, MA: Harvard University Press.

Garcia, E. E. (2001). *Hispanic education in the United States: Raíces y alas*. Lanham, MD: Rowman & Littlefield.

Garcia, M. T. (1991). *Mexican Americans: Leadership, ideology, and identity, 1930–1960*. New Haven, CT: Yale University Press.

Garcia Coll, C., & Szalacha, L. A. (1996). An integrative model for the study of developmental competencies in minority children. *Child Development 67*(5), 1891–1914.

Gee, J. (1996). *Social linguistics and literacies: Ideology in discourses* (2nd ed.). London, England: Routledge Falmer.

Gent, M. J. (2009). On-campus service projects: An experiment in education for liberation. *Organization Management Journal, 6*(3), 166–177.

Gibbons, P. (2009). *English learners, academic literacy and thinking: Learning in the challenge zone.* Portsmouth, NH: Heinemann.

Gilligan, C., Brown, L. M., & Rogers, A. (1988). *Psyche-embedded: A place for body, relationships, and culture in personality theory.* Cambridge, MA: Harvard Project on Women's Psychology and Girls' Development.

Glass, R., & Wong, P. (2003, Spring). Engaged pedagogy: Meeting the demands for justice in urban professional development schools. *Teacher Education Quarterly, 30*(2), 69–87.

Goldhaber, D., & Anthony, E. (2003). *Teacher quality and student achievement.* New York, NY: Teachers College Press. (Eric Document Reproduction Service No. ED477271)

Goldhaber, D., & Hansen, M. (2008). *Race, gender and teacher testing: How objective a tool is teacher licensure testing?* (CRPE Working Paper No. 2008-2). Seattle, WA: Center on Reinventing Public Education.

Goldstein, B. S. C. (1995). Critical pedagogy in bilingual special education classroom. *Journal of Learning Disabilities, 28*(8), 463–475.

Gonzales, S. M. (2015). *Abuelita* epistemologies: Counteracting subtractive schools in American education, *Journal of Latinos in Education, 14*(1), 40–54.

González, N. (1995). The funds of knowledge for teaching project. *Practicing Anthropology, 17*(3), 3–6.

González, N., Moll, L., & Amanti, C. (Eds.), (2005). *Funds of knowledge: Theorizing practices in households, communities, and classrooms.* Mahwah, NJ: Erlbaum.

González, N., Moll, L. C., Floyd-Tenery, M., Rivera, A., Rendón, P., Gonzales, R., & Amanti, C. (1993). *Teacher research on funds of knowledge: Learning from households* (Educational Practice Report 6). Santa Cruz, CA: National Center for Research on Cultural Diversity and Second Language Learning, University of California, Santa Cruz.

Goodman, K. S. (1976). Reading: A psycholinguistic guessing game. In H. Singer & R. B. Ruddell (Eds.), *Theoretical models and processes of reading* (pp. 497–508). Newark, DE: International Reading Association.

Goodman, K. S. (1982). *Language and literacy: Selected readings of Kenneth S. Goodman.* Boston, MA: Routledge, Kegan & Paul.

Goodman, K. S. (1996). *On reading.* Portsmouth, NH: Heinemann.

Goodman, K. S., & Goodman, Y. (2013). *Making sense of learners making sense of written language: The selected works of Kenneth S. Goodman and Yetta M. Goodman.* New York, NY: Routledge.

Gouvea, A. (1998). *From critical pedagogy to classroom realities. Reflections on the São Paulo experience.* Unpublished manuscript.

Grant, C. (2008). Teacher capacities. In M. Cochran-Smith, S. Feiman-Nemser, D. J. McIntyre, & K. E. Demers (Eds.), *Handbook of research in teacher education* (pp. 307–330). New York, NY: Routledge/Taylor & Francis Group.

Grant, C. A., & Agosto, V. (2008). Teacher capacity and social justice in teacher education. In M. Cochran-Smith, S. Feiman-Nemser, D. J. McIntyre, & K. E. Demers (Eds.), *Handbook of research in teacher education* (pp. 175–200). New York, NY: Routledge/Taylor & Francis Group.

Greene, M. (1988). *The dialectic of freedom.* New York, NY: Teachers College Press.

Guitiérrez, K. D., & Rogoff, B. (2003). Cultural ways of learning: Individual traits or repertoires of practice. *Educational Researcher, 32*(5), 19–25.

Gutierrez-Gomez, C. (2007). The need for highly qualified teachers. In L. Díaz Soto (Ed.), *The Praeger handbook of Latino education in the U.S.* (Vol. 2, pp. 331–337). Westport, CT: Praeger.

Gursky, D. (2002). Recruiting minority teachers. *The Education Digest 67*(8), 28–34.

Gutstein, R. (2006). The real world as we have seen it: Latino/a parents' voices on teaching mathematics for social justice. *Mathematical Thinking and Learning, 8*(3), 331–358.

Haberman, M. (2005). *Star teachers: The ideology of best practice of effective teachers of diverse children and youth in poverty.* Houston, TX: Haberman Educational Foundation.

Hernandez, I. (1993). Foreword. In P. Riley (Ed.), *Growing up Native American* (pp. 7–16). New York, NY: Avon.

Herrera, S. C., Perez, D. R., & Escamilla, K. (2011). *Teaching reading to English language learners.* Boston, MA: Allyn & Bacon.

Hidalgo, N. M. (2000). Puerto Rican mothering strategies: The role of mothers and grandmothers in promoting school success. In S. Nieto (Ed.), *Puerto Rican students in U.S. schools* (pp. 167–196). Mahwah, NJ: LEA.

hooks, b. (1984). *Feminist theory: From margin to center.* Cambridge, MA: South End Press.

hooks, b. (1994). *Teaching to transgress: Education as the practice of freedom.* New York, NY: Routledge.

Huerta, T. M., & Brittain, C. M. (2010). Effective practices that matter for Latino children. In E. G. Murrillo, Jr. (Ed.), *Handbook of Latinos in education* (pp. 382–389). New York, NY: Routledge.

Hurtado, A. (1996). *The color of privilege: Three blasphemies on race and feminism.* Ann Arbor, MI: The University of Michigan Press.

Interstate Teacher Assessment and Support Network. (2010). *Model core standards: A resource for state dialogue.* Washington, DC: Council of Chief State School Officers.

Inter-University Program for Latino Research. (2015). *About IUPLR.* Retrieved from http://iuplr.nd.edu/about/

Irizarry, J. (2011). *The Latinization of U.S. schools: Successful teaching and learning in shifting cultural contexts.* Boulder, CO: Paradigm Publishers.

Jahn, J., & Grene, M. (1961). *Muntu: African culture and the Western world.* New York, NY: Grove Press, Inc.

Keating, A. (2009). *The Gloria Anzaldúa reader.* Durham, NC: Duke University Press.

Kellner, D. (2000). Globalization and new social movements: Lessons for critical theory and pedagogy. In N. C. Burbules & C. A. Torres (Eds.), *Globalization and education: Critical Perspectives* (pp. 299–321). New York, NY: Routledge.

Kennedy, J. F. (1962, June 11). *Commencement address, Yale University.* Retrieved from http://www.presidency.ucsb.edu/ws/?pid=29661

Klein, M. (2007). Peace education and Paulo Freire's method: Towards the democratisation of teaching and learning. *Convergence, 40*(2), 187–203.

Kirby, S. N., Berends, M., & Naftel, S. (1999). Supply and demand of minority teacher in Texas: Problems and prospects. *Education Evaluation and Policy Analysis, 21*(1), 47–66.

Kohn, A. (2015, August 16). The perils of "growth mindset" education: Why we're trying to fix our kids when we should be fixing the system. *Salon Magazine.* Retrieved from http://www.salon.com/2015/08/16/the_education_fad_thats_hurting_our_kids_what_you_need_to_know_about_growth_mindset_theory_and_the_harmful_lessons_it_imparts/

Krogstad, J. M. (2014). *A view of the future through kindergarten demographics*. Retrieved from Pew Research Center website: http://www.pewresearch.org/fact-tank/2014/07/08/a-view-of-the-future-through-kindergarten-demographics

Ladson-Billings, G. (2005). Is the team all right? Diversity in teacher education. *Journal of Teacher Education, 56*(3), 229–234.

Lara, I. (2002). Healing Sueños for academia. In G. Anzaldúa & A. Keating (Eds.), *This bridge we call home: Radical visions for transformation* (pp. 433–438). New York, NY: Routledge.

Lavadenz, M. (1996). Authentic assessment: Toward equitable assessment of language minority students. *New Schools, New Communities, 12*(2), 31–35.

Lee, J., & Zhou, M. (2014). The success frame and achievement paradox: The costs and consequences for Asian Americans. *Race and Social Problems, 6*(1), 38–55.

LeDoux, J. (1998). *The emotional brain: The mysterious underpinnings of emotional life*. New York, NY: Simon and Schuster.

Lipkin, A. (1999). *Understanding homosexuality, changing schools*. Boulder, CO: Westview Press.

López, P. D., & Valenzuela, A. (2014). Resisting epistemological exclusion and inserting La Clase Mágica into state-level policy discourses. In B. Flores, O. Vasquez, & E. R. Clark (Eds.), *La Clase Mágica: Generating transworld pedagogy* (pp. 76–98). Lanham, MD: Lexington Publishers, Rowman Littlefield Publishing Group.

López, P. D., Valenzuela, A., & Garcia, E. (2011). The critical ethnography for public policy. In B. Levinson & M. Pollock (Eds.), *Companion to the anthropology of education* (pp. 547–563). Maiden, MA: Wiley-Blackwell.

Luna, J. M. (2011). *Danza Mexica: Indigenous identity, spirituality, activism and performance*. (Unpublished doctoral dissertation). University of California, Davis, Davis, CA.

Macedo, D., Dendrinos, B., & Gounari, P. (2003). *The hegemony of English*. Boulder, CO: Paradigm Publishers.

Mannheim, K. (1923/1952). The problem of generations. In P. Kecskemeti (Ed.), *Karl Mannheim, essays on the sociology of knowledge* (pp. 276–322). London, England: Routledge & Kegan Paul. (Original work published 1923)

Mariategui, J. C. (1928/1971). *Seven interpretative essays on Peruvian reality.* Austin, TX: University of Texas Press. (Original work published 1928)

Matias, C. E. (2013). Tears worth telling: Urban teaching and the possibilities of racial justice, *Multicultural Perspectives, 15*(4), 187–193.

McIntosh, P. (1990, Winter). White privilege: Unpacking the invisible knapsack. *Independent School,* 31–36.

Medina, J. (2008). *Brain rules: 12 principles for surviving and thriving at work, home and school.* Seattle, WA: Pear Press.

Meier, K. J., Eller, W. S., Wrinkle, R. D., & Polinard, J. L. (2001). Zen and the art of policy analysis: A response to Nielsen and Wolf. *Journal of Politics, 63*(2), 616–629.

Meier, K. J., & Smith, K. B. (1994, December). Representative democracy and representative bureaucracy. *Social Science Quarterly, 75,* 798–803.

Meier, K. J., & Stewart, J. (1991). *The politics of Hispanic education.* Albany, NY: State University of New York Press.

Meier, K. J., Wrinkle, R. D., & Polinard, J. L. (1999, November). Representative bureaucracy and distributional equity: Addressing the hard question. *Journal of Politics, 61,* 1025–1039.

Meltzer, J., & Hamann, E. T. (2005). *Meeting the development needs of English language learners through literacy instruction. Part 2: Focus on classroom teaching and learning strategies* (Paper 53, faculty publications). Lincoln, NE: University of Nebraska–Lincoln, Department of Teaching, Learning and Teacher Education. Retrieved from http://digitalcommons.unl.edu/teachlearnfacpub/53

Mendoza Reis, N., & Flores, B. (2014). Changing the pedagogical culture of schools with Latino English language learners: Reculturing instructional leadership. In P. R. Portes, S. Salas, P. Baquedano-López, & P. J. Mellom (Eds.), *U.S. Latinos in K–12 education: Seminal research-based policy directions for change we can believe in* (pp. 192–203). Charlotte, NC: Information Age Publishing.

Menken, K. (2008). *English learners left behind: Standardized testing as language policy.* Clevedon, England: Multilingual Matters.

Mercado, C. I. (2001). The learner: Race, ethnicity, and linguistic difference. In V. Richardson (Ed.), *Handbook of research on teaching* (4th ed., pp. 668–691). Washington, DC: American Educational Research Association.

Mercado, C. I. (2012). Recruiting and preparing teachers for New York Puerto Rican communities: A historical, public policy perspective. *CENTRO: Journal of the Center for Puerto Rican Studies, 24*(2), 110–139.

Mercado, C. I., & Brochin-Ceballos, C. (2011). Growing quality teachers: Community-oriented preparation. In B. B. Flores, R. H. Sheets, & E. R. Clark (Eds.), *Teacher preparation for bilingual student populations: Educar para transformer.* New York, NY: Taylor and Francis/ Routledge.

Mercado, C. I., & Moll, L.C. (1997). The study of funds of knowledge: Collaborative research in Latin@/Puerto Rican homes. *CENTRO: Journal of the Center for Puerto Rican Studies, 9*(9), 26–42.

Mercado, C. I., & Reyes, L. O. (2010). Latino community activism in the 21st century. In E.G. Murillo, Jr. (Ed.), *Handbook of Latinos in education* (pp. 250–261). New York, NY: Routledge.

Merino, B. J., Trueba, E. T., & Samaniego, F. A. (Eds.). (1993). *Language and culture in learning: Teaching Spanish to native speakers of Spanish.* New York, NY: Routledge.

Mireles, J. G., & Cotera, M. E. (2006). *Life along the border: A landmark Tejana thesis.* College Station, TX: Texas A&M University Press.

Moll, L. C. (1992). *Vygotsky and education: Instructional implications and applications of sociohistorical psychology.* Cambridge, England: Cambridge University Press.

Moll, L. C. (1998). Turning to the world: Bilingual schooling, literacy, and the cultural mediation of thinking. In T. Shanahan & F. V. Rodriguez Brown (Eds.), *47th yearbook of the National Reading Conference* (pp. 59–75). Chicago, IL: National Reading Conference.

Moll, L. C., & Amanti, C. (Eds.). (2005). *Funds of knowledge: Theorizing practices in households, communities, and classrooms* (pp. 1–27). Mahwah, NJ: Lawrence Erlbaum.

Moll, L. C., & González, N. (2004). Engaging life: A funds of knowledge approach to multicultural education. In J. A. Banks & C. A. M. Banks (Eds.), *Handbook of research on multicultural education* (2nd ed., pp. 699–715). San Francisco, CA: Jossey-Bass.

Moll, L. C., González, N., Amanti, C., & Neff, D. (1992). Funds of knowledge for teaching: A qualitative approach to connect households and classrooms. *Theory into Practice, 31*(2), 132–141.

Moll, L. C., & Greenberg, J. B. (1990). Creating zones of possibilities: Combining social contexts for instruction. In L. C. Moll (Ed.), *Vygotsky and education: Instructional implications and applications of sociohistorical psychology* (pp. 319–348). Cambridge, England: Cambridge University Press.

Moraga, C., & Anzaldúa, G. (1981). *This bridge called my back: Writings by radical women of color*. Watertown, MA: Persephone Press.

Moreno Sandoval, C. D. (2013). Critical ancestral computing: A culturally relevant computer science education. *PsychNology Journal, 11*(1), 91–112.

Murphey, D., Guzman, L., & Torres, A. M. (2014). *America's Hispanic children: Gaining ground, looking forward*. Retrieved from Child Trends website: http://www.childtrends.org/wp-content/uploads/2014/09/2014-38AmericaHispanicChildren.pdf

National Center for Education Statistics. (2014). *Teacher trends*. Retrieved from http://nces.ed.gov/fastfacts/display.asp?id=28

National Clearinghouse for English Language Acquisition and Language Instruction Educational Programs. (2007). *The growing numbers of limited English proficient students: 1995/96– 2005/06*. Retrieved from http://www.ncela.us/files/uploads/4/GrowingLEP_0506.pdf

National Council for Accreditation of Teacher Education. (2008). *Unit standards in effect 2008*. Washington, DC: Author. Retrieved from http://www.ncate.org/Standards/UnitStandards/UnitStandardsinEffect2008/tabid/476/Default.aspx

National Council of Teachers of English. (2013). *Formative assessment that truly informs instruction*. Retrieved from http://www.ncte.org/library/NCTEFiles/Resources/Positions/formative-assessment_single.pdf

National Latino Education Research Agenda Project. (2003). *Education research framework and agenda*. New York, NY: Research Foundation, City University of New York.

Nielsen, L., & Wolf, P. (1999). *Representative bureaucracy and harder questions: A response to Meier, Wrinkle, and Polinard*. Retrieved from Society for Political Methodology website: http://www.polmeth.wustl.edu/media/Paper/nielse00.pdf.

Nieto, S. (1996). *Affirming diversity: The sociopolitical context of multicultural education* (2nd ed.). White Plains, NY: Longman.

Nieto, S. (2005). Schools for a new majority: The role of teacher education in hard times. *The New Educator, 1*(1), 27–43.

Nieto, S., Rivera, M., Quiñones S., & Irizarry, J. (Eds.). (2012). Charting a new course: Understanding the sociocultural, political, economic, and historical context of Latino/a education in the United States [Special issue]. *Association of Mexican-American Educators (AMAE) Journal, 6*(1).

Oakes, J., & Saunders, M. (2008). Multiple pathways: Promising to prepare all high school students for college, career, and civic participation. In J. Oakes & M. Saunders (Eds.), *Beyond tracking: Multiple pathways to college, career, and civic participation* (pp. 251–268). Cambridge, MA: Harvard Education Press.

Oliva, M., & Staudt, K. (2003). Pathways to teaching: Latino student choice and professional identity development in a teacher training magnet program. *Equity & Excellence in Education, 36*, 270–279.

Orfield, G., Losen, D., Wald, J., & Swanson, C. (2004). *Losing our future: How minority youth are being left behind by the graduation rate crisis.* Cambridge, MA: The Civil Rights Project at Harvard University.

Ortiz, S. (1993). The language we know. In P. Riley (Ed.), *Growing up Native American* (pp. 29–38). New York, NY: Avon.

O'Shea, E. Z. (1935/2000). *El mesquite: A story of the early Spanish settlements between the Nueces and the Rio Grande as told by "La Posta del Palo Alto."* College Station, TX: Texas A & M University Press. (Original work published 1935)

Pandya, J. Z. (2011). *Overtested: How high-stakes accountability fails English language learners.* New York, NY: Teachers College Press.

Pea, R. (2009, June). *Fostering learning in the networked world: Trends, opportunities and challenges for learning environments and education.* Keynote speech at the Third Redesigning Pedagogy International Conference, National Institute of Education, Singapore.

Peckham, I. (2003). Freirean codifications: Changing walls into windows. *Pedagogy 3*(2), 227–244.

Pedraza, P., & Rivera, M. (2005). *Latino education: An agenda for community action research: A volume of the National Latino/a Education Research and Policy Project.* Philadelphia, PA: Lawrence Erlbaum Associates.

Pert, C. (1997). *Molecules of emotion: The science behind mind-body medicine.* New York, NY: Scribner.

Pilcher, J. (1994). Mannheim's sociology of generations: An undervalued legacy. *British Journal of Sociology, 45*(3), 481–495.

Pink, D. (2006). *A whole new mind: Why right-brainers will rule the future.* New York, NY: Riverhead.

Pizarro, M. (1998). Contesting dehumanization: Chicano/a spiritualization, revolutionary possibility, and the curriculum. *Aztlan, 23*(1), 55–76.

Plecki, M., & Loeb, H. (2004). Lessons for policy design and implementation: Examining state and federal efforts to improve teacher quality. *Yearbook of the National Society for the Study of Education, 103*(1), 348–389.

Ponce de Leon Paiva, A. (1992). *Y...El anciano habló* [And...The elder spoke]. Cusco, Peru: J.C. Editors.

Popham, J. (2009, March/April). Unlearned lessons: Six stumbling blocks to our schools' success. *Harvard Education Letter, 25*(2), 6–7.

Public Science Project. (2012). *Participatory action research as public science.* Retrieved http://publicscienceproject.org/

Quiocho, A., & Rios, F. (2000). The power of their presence: Minority group teachers and schooling. *Review of Educational Research, 70*(4), 485–528.

Ranney, S., Schornack, M., Maguire, C., & Dillard-Paltrineri, E. (2014, Spring). Academic language demands: Texts, tasks, and levels of language. *Minnetesol Journal.* Retrieved from http://minnetesoljournal.org/spring-2014/academic-language-demands-texts-tasks-and-levels-of-language

Renner, A., Brown, M., Steins, G., & Burton, S. (2010). A reciprocal global education? Working towards a more humanizing pedagogy through critical literacy. *Intercultural Education, 21*(1), 41–54.

Reyes, M., & Halcón, J. J. (2001). *The best for our children: Critical perspectives on literacy for Latino students.* New York, NY: Teachers College Press.

Riley, P. (1993). *Growing up Native American.* New York, NY: Avon.

Rivera, M., Medellín-Paz, C., & Pedraza, P. (2010). *Imagination for the imagined nation. A creative justice approach to learning.* New York, NY: Center for Puerto Rican Studies, Hunter College, City University of New York.

Rivera, M., & Pedraza, P. (2000). The spirit of transformation: An education reform movement in a New York City Latino community. In S. Nieto (Ed.), *Puerto Rican students in U.S. schools* (pp. 223–243). Mahwah, NJ: Lawrence Erlbaum Associates.

Roberts, P. (1994). Education, dialogue and intervention: Revisiting the Freirean project. *Educational Studies, 20*(3), 307–328.

Roberts, P. (1998). Extending literate horizons: Paulo Freire and the multidimensional word. *Educational Review, 50*(2), 105–114.

Rogers, A., Casey, M., Ekert, J., Holland, J., Nakkula, V., & Sheinberg, N. (1999). An interpretive poetics of languages of the unsayable. In R. Josselson & A. Lieblich (Eds.), *Making meaning of narratives: The narrative study of lives* (pp. 77–106). Thousand Oaks, CA: Sage.

Romano-V, O. I. (1967). Minorities, history and the cultural mystique. *El Grito, 1*(1), 5–11.

Santa Ana, O. (2002). *Brown tide rising: Metaphors of Latinos in contemporary American public discourse.* Austin, TX: University of Texas Press.

Shirts, G. R. (1993). *BaFa BaFa.* Retrieved from Simulation Training Systems website: http://www.SimulationTrainingSystems.com

Short, D. J., & Fitzsimmons, S. (2007). *Double the work: Challenges and solutions to acquiring language and academic literacy for adolescent English language learners—a report commissioned by the Carnegie Corporation of New York.* Washington, DC: Alliance for Excellent Education.

Shulman, L. S. (1986). Those who understand: Knowledge growth in teaching. *Educational Researcher, 15*(2), 4–14.

Shulman, L. S. (2005, Spring). Pedagogies of uncertainty. *Liberal Education, Newsletter of the Association of American Colleges and Universities.* Retrieved from http://www.aacu.org/liberaleducation/le-sp05/le-sp05feature2.cfm

Simmons, W. (2011, Fall). *Smart education systems: Community-centered school reform.* Retrieved from Annenberg Institute for School Reform website: http://annenberginstitute.org/about/smart-education-systems

Skinner, E., Garreton, M. T., & Schultz, B. D. (2011). *Grow your own teachers: Grassroots change for teacher education.* New York, NY: Teachers College Press.

Sleeter, C. E. (2011). *The academic and social value of ethnic studies: A research review.* Washington, DC: National Education Association.

Solórzano, D., & Yosso, T. J. (2002). Critical race methodology: Counter-storytelling as an analytical framework for education research. *Qualitative Inquiry, 8*(1), 23–44.

Sosa, T., & Gomez, K. (2012). Connecting teacher efficacy beliefs in promoting resilience to support of Latino students. *Urban Education, 47,* 876–909.

Sousa, D. (2011). *How the brain learns.* Thousand Oaks, CA: Corwin Press.

Stanton-Salazar, R. D. (1997). A social capital framework for understanding the socialization of racial minority children and youth. *Harvard Educational Review, 67*(1), 1–40.

Tafolla, C. (2014). Our abuelos, the trees. In *This river here: Poems of San Antonio.* San Antonio, TX: Wings Press.

Torre, M. E. (2009). Participatory action research and critical race theory: Fueling spaces for *nos-otras* to research. *Urban Review, 41*(1), 106–120.

Torre, M. E., & Ayala J. (2009). Envisioning participatory action research *entremundos. Feminism & Psychology, 19*(3), 387–393.

Torre, M. E., Fine, M., Alexander, N., Billups, A., Blanding, Y., Genao, E., . . . Salah, T. (2008). Participatory action research in the contact zone. In J. Cammarota & M. Fine (Eds.), *Revolutionizing education: Youth participatory action research in motion* (pp. 23–43). New York, NY: Routledge.

Torres, M. N., & Reyes, L. V. (2011). *Research as praxis: Democratizing education epistemologies.* New York, NY: Peter Lang.

Tyack, D., & Cuban, L. (1995). *Tinkering toward utopia: A century of public school reform.* Cambridge, MA: Harvard University Press.

United Federation of Teachers Committee on Social and Economic Justice. (2008). *Draft resolution on the disappearing Black and Latino educator.* Retrieved from http://www.ice-uft.org/seanahern-resolution.htm

Urrieta, L. (2009). *Working from within: Chicana and Chicano activist educators in whitestream schools.* Tucson, AZ: University of Arizona Press.

U.S. Census Bureau. (2010, May 17). *Most children younger than age 1 are minorities, Census Bureau reports.* Retrieved from http://www.census .gov/newsroom/releases/archives/population/cb12-90.html

Valdés, G. (1996). *Con respeto: Bridging the distances between culturally diverse families and schools.* New York, NY: Teachers College Press.

Valenzuela, A. (1999). *Subtractive schooling: U.S.-Mexican youth and the politics of caring.* Albany, NY: State University of New York Press.

Valenzuela, A. (Ed.). (2005). *Leaving children behind: How "Texas-style" accountability fails Latino youth.* Albany, NY: State University of New York Press.

Valenzuela, A. (2008). Uncovering internalized oppression. In M. Pollock (Ed.), *Everyday antiracism: Concrete strategies for successfully navigating the relevance of race in school* (pp. 50–55). New York, NY: The New Press.

Valenzuela, A. (2010, February 4). "Avatar," race, and epistemology [Web log post]. Retrieved from http://texasedequity.blogspot.com/2010/01/my-review-of-avatar-epistemology-and.html

Valenzuela, A. (2012). Reflection on age and generation: Last weekend's Raza Unida Party reunion in Austin. *Rio Grande Guardian.* Retrieved from http://www.riograndeguardian.com/archives_results.asp

Valenzuela, A., & López, P. D. (2014). Cultivating a cadre of critically conscious teachers and "Taking this country to a totally new place." In P. Portes, S. Salas, & P. Mellom (Eds.), *U.S. Latinos in K–12 education: Seminal research-based policy directions for change we can believe in* (pp. 35–44). Charlotte, NC: Information Age Publishing.

Valenzuela, A., & López, P. D. (2015). A concise history of the National Latino/a Education Research and Policy Project: Origins, identity, accomplishments and initiatives. In A. Colon-Muñiz & M. Lavadenz (Eds.), *Latino civil rights in education: La lucha sigue* (pp. 188–193). Boulder, CO: Paradigm Publishers.

Valenzuela, A., Zamora, E., & Rubio, B. (2015). Academia Cuauhtli and the eagle: Danza Mexica and the epistemology of the circle. *Voices in Urban Education, 41.* Retrieved from http://vue.annenberginstitute.org/issues/41/academia-cuauhtli-and-eagle-danza-mexica-and-epistemology-circle

Villegas, A. M. (2007). *Profile of new Hispanic teachers in U.S. public schools: Looking at issues of quantity and quality.* Paper presented at the Annual Meeting of the American Education Research Association, Chicago, IL.

Villegas, A. M. (2009). *Hispanic research agenda: Teacher preparation.* Paper presented at the Board Meeting of the National Latino/a Education Research Agenda Project (NLERAP), Ford Foundation, New York, NY.

Villegas, A. M., & Clewell, B. C. (1998). Increasing teacher diversity by tapping the paraprofessional pool. *Theory into Practice, 37*(2), 121–130.

Villegas, A. M., & Irvine, J. J. (2010). Diversifying the teaching force: An examination of major arguments. *The Urban Review, 42*(3), 175–192.

Villegas, A. M., & Lucas, T. (2001). *Educating culturally responsive teachers: A coherent approach.* Albany, NY: State University of New York Press.

Villegas, A. M., & Lucas, T. (2002). Preparing culturally responsive teachers rethinking the curriculum. *Journal of Teacher Education, 53*(1), 20–32.

Villenas, S. A. (2009). Knowing and unknowing transnational Latino lives in teacher education: At the intersection of educational research and the Latino humanities. *The High School Journal, 92*(4), 129–136.

Vygotsky, L. S. (1978). *Mind and society: The development of higher mental processes.* Cambridge, MA: Harvard University Press.

Wang, C. C., Wu, K. Y., Tao, Z. W., & Carovano, K. (1998). PhotoVoice as a participatory health promotion strategy. *Health Promotion International, 13*(1), 75–86.

Warren, M. R., & Mapp, K. L. (2011). *A match on dry grass: Community organizing as a catalyst for school reform.* New York, NY: Oxford University Press.

Weisner, T. S. (2002). Ecocultural understanding of children's developmental pathways. *Human Development, 45,* 275–281.

Wilson, S. (2008). *Research is ceremony: Indigenous research methods.* Black Point, Nova Scotia: Fernwood Publishing Co.

Wong Filmore, L., & Snow, C. (2000). *What teachers need to know about language.* Washington, DC: ERIC Clearinghouse on Languages and Linguistics.

Yosso, T. J. (2005). Whose culture has capital? A critical race theory discussion of community cultural wealth. *Race Ethnicity and Education, 8*(1), 69–91.

Yosso, T. J. (2006). *Critical race counterstories along the Chicana/Chicano educational pipeline.* New York, NY: Routledge.

Zamora, E. (2008). *Claiming rights and righting wrongs in Texas: Mexican workers and job politics during World War II.* College Station, TX: Texas A&M Press.

Zamora, E. (2014). *The World War I diary of José de la Luz Sáenz.* College Station, TX: Texas A&M Press.

Zull, J. (2002). *The art of changing the brain: Enriching the practice of teaching by exploring the biology of learning.* Sterling, VA: Stylus.

Zwiers, J. (2008). *Building academic language: Essential practices for content classrooms.* San Francisco, CA: Jossey-Bass.

Index

About the Editor and Contributors

Adele Arellano has been a professor in the College of Education at CSU Sacramento since 1998. Her research, professional learning, and teaching foci have been in the areas of second-language acquisition, bilingualism and content/disciplinary literacy, particularly as they relate to designing and providing effective instruction for English learners in the secondary classroom. She currently teachers methodology courses in integrated and designated ELD and adolescent academic and disciplinary literacy for preservice secondary candidates in the CSU's single-subject credential program and serves on the steering committee for the Expository Reading and Writing Course (ERWC) program sponsored by the CSU Chancellor's Office.

Jennifer Ayala, Ph.D., is associate professor in the School of Education at Saint Peter's University in Jersey City, New Jersey. She has worked on participatory action research projects with high school and college age youth. Past work has focused on Latino/a mother-daughter relationships, youth voice in education policy, PAR processes in and outside the classroom, and Latino/a experiences in higher education. Recent publications include: "'Why Don't We Learn Like This in School?' One Participatory Action Research Collective's Framework for Developing Policy Thinking" with M. Zaal in *Journal for Curriculum Theorizing;* and "Creative Expressions of Agency: Contemplating Youth Voice and Adult Roles in Participatory Action Research" with V. Jones, C. Stewart, and A. Galletta in *National Society for the Study of Education Yearbooks: Student Voice in American Educational Policy, 114*(1) (2015).

Margarita Ines Berta-Avila is a professor in the College of Education at Sacramento State University. She received her doctorate in International and Multicultural Education in the School of Education at the University of San Francisco. She majored in Chicana/o Studies from the University of California, Davis, and pursued a M.A. in Education and a teaching credential from Claremont Graduate University. Currently, Dr. Berta-Avila teaches courses on curriculum development and social political foundations in education. Dr. Berta-Avila is active in testifying at the Capitol and/or other venues with respect to access and equity in education for English language learners, students of color, and/or other marginalized communities. In addition, Dr. Berta-Avila pursues her scholarly work within the areas of participatory action research, critical pedagogy/social justice education, and Chicana/o educators in the field. In collaboration with Dr. Julie Figueroa and Dr. Anita Tijerina-Revilla, an edited volume titled *Marching Students: Chicana/o Activism in Education, 1968 to the Present* was released in the spring of 2011.

Julio Cammarota is an associate professor of multicultural education at Iowa State University. His research focuses on participatory action research with Latino/a youth, institutional factors in academic achievement, and liberatory pedagogy. He has published articles on family, work, and education among Latino/as and on the relationship between culture and academic achievement. Dr Cammarota's work has been instrumental with advancing social justice in education and youth development. He is the coeditor of two volumes in the Critical Youth Studies series published by Routledge/Falmer Press: *Beyond Resistance! Youth Activism and Community Change: New Democratic Possibilities for Practice and Policy for America's Youth* (2006) and *Revolutionizing Education: Youth Participatory Action Research in Motion* (2008). In addition, Dr. Cammarota has published an ethnography of Latino/a youth entitled *Sueños Americanos: Barrio Youth Negotiate Social and Cultural Identities* (2008). His latest work includes coediting a volume on the struggle for ethnic studies in Tucson, Arizona: *Raza Studies: The Public Option for Educational Revolution* (2014).

José Cintrón is professor of Education at California State University, Sacramento, College of Education, Teaching Credentials Branch and past chair of the Bilingual/Multicultural Education Department. Currently he teaches educational foundations and multicultural education and introduction to English Learner courses in the Single Subject B/CLAD (Bilingual/Culture Language Academic Development) credential program. In addition, he teaches an advanced bilingualism/sociolinguistics course in the Multicultural Masters program. Dr. Cintrón received the Ph.D. (1985) from the University of California, Santa Bárbara, in Educational Psychology with specialization in Bilingual and Cross-Cultural

Education. He has a B.A and M.A.T. in Spanish from Purdue University. His academic interests include critical/multicultural education theory and curriculum integration, bilingual education, sociolinguistics, precredential teacher preparation, urban education, and school/classroom ethnography. Dr. Cintrón is the West Coast Regional Director of the National Latino Education Research and Policy (NLERAP) Project—Teacher Education Institute. This multistate effort is administered at the University of Texas, Austin.

Barbara Flores is a pioneer Latina scholar activist, teacher educator, children's literature writer, and international expert in the areas of biliteracy development, teaching/learning based on Vygotsky's sociocultural theoretical framework, professional staff development, bilingual education, and critical pedagogy. She has published her work in professional journals, books, and chapters as well as lectured throughout the United States, Mexico, Central America, South America, the Caribbean, Canada, New Zealand, and Australia. She has been a professor for the last 35 years and is currently semiretired from California State University, San Bernardino. She has been a school board member for San Bernardino City Unified School District since 2008 and currently president of the California Latino School Boards Association and director of Community Affairs for the California Association of Bilingual Education.

Carmen I. Mercado's life trajectory took an unexpected turn in 1969, a time when Puerto Ricans, the largest Spanish-speaking student population, was not faring well in local schools. Recruited through an alternative pathway, her circumstantial bilingualism opened doors at a new, open-walled, dual-language school in one of the poorest neighborhoods in the city. The joys and challenges of learning to teach in community, with community, and for community, has shaped her life, defined her purpose as an educator, and influenced her "nontraditional" practice in mainstream teacher education. Now retired, she writes to explore what constitutes quality in teacher preparation and to disrupt the impact of ill-conceived policies that affect the preparation of teachers, such as No Child Left Behind. She draws on data from years of teaching as research and collaborative literacy research in local homes and communities to inform practice and policy on new educator preparation.

Melissa Rivera, Ph.D., is a scholar whose work focuses on connection, creativity, and change in learning and leadership contexts. For the past 20 years she has been dedicated to collaborating on participatory action research initiatives with public schools and universities, community-based organizations, entrepreneurial companies, and a women's maximum-security prison. Her research is grounded in psychology (developmental, women's, somatic, and positive), critical and feminist theories, creativity studies, and conscious activism. She has codeveloped programs and publications with young people, educators, entrepreneurs, artists, and activists on personal transformation, community development, and social justice, including *Latino Education: An Agenda for Community Action Research*, 2006 (edited with Pedro Pedraza) and *PAR Entremundos: A Pedagogy for the Americas* (forthcoming). Her undergraduate and doctoral degrees are from Brown University and Harvard Graduate School of Education, respectively.

Louie F. Rodríguez is an associate professor and co-director of the Doctorate in Educational Leadership at California State University, San Bernardino (CSUSB). His research and scholarship focuses on equity issues, namely how institutional culture shapes students' experiences in urban schools. He is the author of three books including *Intentional Excellence: The Pedagogy, Power, and Politics of Excellence in Latina/o Schools and Communities* (2015), *The Time is Now: Understanding and Responding to the Black and Latina/o Dropout Crisis in the U.S.* (2014), and *Small Schools and Urban Youth* (2008). He has also published widely on Latino/a education, educational policy, and students' experiences in public schools. In 2014 he was named an "Emerging Leader" by Phi Delta Kappa in Washington, DC, and in 2015 he was recognized as Outstanding Latino/a Faculty of the Year by the American Association of Hispanics in Higher Education. He earned his master's and doctorate in education from Harvard.

Angela Valenzuela is a professor in both the Educational Policy and Planning Program Area within the Department of Educational Administration and the Cultural Studies in Education Program within the Department of Curriculum and Instruction at the University of Texas at Austin, where she also serves as the director of the University of Texas Center for Education Policy. A Stanford University graduate, her previous teaching positions were in Sociology at Rice University in Houston, Texas (1990–98), as well as a Visiting Scholar at the Center for Mexican American Studies at the University of Houston (1998–99). In 2007, as a Fulbright Scholar she taught in the College of Law at the University of Guanajuato in Mexico. Valenzuela is also the author of award-winning book, *Subtractive Schooling: U.S.–Mexican Youth and the Politics of Caring* (1999) and *Leaving Children Behind: How "Texas-Style" Accountability Fails Latino Youth* (2004). Valenzuela's research and teaching interests are in the sociology of education, race and ethnic relations, education policy, school partnerships, urban education reform, and indigenous education.